Oil/Water Separation: State of the Art

U.S. Environmental Protection Agency

United States
Environmental Protection
Agency

Industrial Environmental
Research Laboratory
Cincinnati OH 45268

EPA-600/2-78-069
April 1978

Research and Development

♻EPA

Oil/Water Separation:
State of the Art

Environmental Protection
Technology Series

RESEARCH REPORTING SERIES

Research reports of the Office of Research and Development, U.S. Environmental Protection Agency, have been grouped into nine series. These nine broad categories were established to facilitate further development and application of environmental technology. Elimination of traditional grouping was consciously planned to foster technology transfer and a maximum interface in related fields. The nine series are:

1. Environmental Health Effects Research
2. Environmental Protection Technology
3. Ecological Research
4. Environmental Monitoring
5. Socioeconomic Environmental Studies
6. Scientific and Technical Assessment Reports (STAR)
7. Interagency Energy-Environment Research and Development
8. "Special" Reports
9. Miscellaneous Reports

This report has been assigned to the ENVIRONMENTAL PROTECTION TECH-NOLOGY series. This series describes research performed to develop and demonstrate instrumentation, equipment, and methodology to repair or prevent environmental degradation from point and non-point sources of pollution. This work provides the new or improved technology required for the control and treatment of pollution sources to meet environmental quality standards.

EPA-600/2-78-069
April 1978

OIL/WATER SEPARATION
STATE-OF-THE-ART

by

Fidelis A. Osamor
Robert C. Ahlert, Ph.D.
Department of Chemical and Biochemical Engineering
Rutgers, The State University of New Jersey
New Brunswick, New Jersey 08903

Grant No. R803978

Project Officer

Leo T. McCarthy, Jr.
Oil & Hazardous Materials Spills Branch
Industrial Environmental Research Laboratory-Cincinnati
Edison, New Jersey 08817

INDUSTRIAL ENVIRONMENTAL RESEARCH LABORATORY
OFFICE OF RESEARCH AND DEVELOPMENT
U.S. ENVIRONMENTAL PROTECTION AGENCY
CINCINNATI, OHIO 45268

DISCLAIMER

This report has been reviewed by the Industrial Environmental Research Laboratory, U.S. Environmental Protection Agency, and approved for publication. Approval does not signify that the contents necessarily reflect the views and policies of the U.S. Environmental Protection Agency, nor does mention of trade names or commercial products constitute endorsement or recommendation for use.

FOREWORD

When energy and material resources are extracted, processed, converted, and used, the related pollutional impacts on our environment and
even on our health often require that new and increasingly more efficient
pollution control methods be used. The Industrial Environmental Research
Laboratory - Cincinnati (IERL - Ci) assists in developing and demonstrating
new and improved methodologies that will meet these needs both efficiently
and economically.

Effluent discharge guidelines for oil have been established for
existing onshore and offshore industries, and performance standards have
been stipulated for new point sources.

This report identifies, organizes, and interprets technical and
commercial literature resources on oil/water separation. As such, this
state-of-the-art report will be most useful to regulatory personnel of
Federal and State agencies in assessing the capabilities of existing
technology to meet standards established for the control of oil discharges.

David G. Stephan
Director
Industrial Environmental Research Laboratory
Cincinnati

ABSTRACT

This report reviews the state-of-the art for oil/water separating devices and processes. Devices and processes are classified according to the primary mechanism that induces separation of oil/water mixtures. The basic concepts, specific design features, operational conditions, and limitations of each category are discussed.

Literature on test evaluation of a variety of devices is critiqued on the basis of actual or potential success in treating various oil/water systems states. No single technique can separate all oil/water system states efficiently. Specific deficiencies in existing technology have been identified.

Reverse osmosis, ultrafiltration, and carbon adsorption possess great potential, but high equipment and operational costs will continue to limit their use for treating oily wastestreams. A combination of devices in a process chain is therefore necessary for production of effluents with desired discharge quality (<10 ppm of oil). The specific characteristics of an oily wastewater determine the combination of devices that will yield required effluent concentrations.

This report was submitted in fulfillment of Research Grant No. R803978 by Rutgers University under the sponsorship of the U.S. Environmental Protection Agency. The report covers the period July 1, 1975, to June 30, 1977, and work was completed as of July 31, 1977.

CONTENTS

FIGURES

TABLES

ACKNOWLEDGEMENTS

The authors are indebted to Frank Freestone and Leo McCarthy of the U.S. Environmental Protection Agency, Edison, New Jersey, for their suggestions and assistance.

SECTION 1

INTRODUCTION

BACKGROUND

The rising demand for energy by a growing population has led to continued increases in world production of crude oil. As an immediate consequence, there is a worsening problem of oil pollution of waterways and the marine environment by discharges of oily wastewaters.

There are various sources of oily substances, and the following key sources have been identified:

a) natural seeps;
b) petroleum mining and refining operations;
c) accidental oil spills;
d) discharges from transporting vessels;
e) discharges from chemical and industrial plants; and
f) stormwater runoff.

The magnitude of the oily waste problem has been described in the literature (Boesch et al., 1974; SCEP, 1970), but data on the amount of the discharge from these key sources are at best speculative.

In response to public demand for a clean environment, laws and regulations have been promulgated. Effluent discharge guidelines have been established for existing onshore and offshore industries, and performance standards have been stipulated for new point sources (U.S. EPA, 1974, 1975).

Industries are approaching oil pollution abatement by process modifications and the use of advanced waste treatment technology for end-of-pipe treatment. Secondary and tertiary recovery methods for crude oil are minimizing the volume of production water generated during production operations. New ship designs, incorporating separate holding tanks for bilge and ballast water, and use of the load-on-top procedure have cut down on the volume of oily wastewater discharged at sea. Separation devices for oil/water mixtures are being installed onboard ships, and there is an increasing number of dockside treatment facilities for bilge and ballast waters. However, large volumes of oily wastewaters must be treated by even more advanced methods to meet effluent standards before discharge into United States waters.

1

OBJECTIVE OF REPORT

Strict pollution control laws place heavy emphasis on the development of economical and reliable devices for separation of oil/water mixtures. The objective of this report is to review the state-of-the-art for oil/water separation devices and processes. The scope of this investigation will be the technology available for shipboard and shoreside treatment of bilge and ballast waters and the oily wastewaters associated with crude oil production. Separation devices will be classified according to the primary mechanism that induces separation of oil/water mixtures. The basic concepts of each class of equipment, specific design features, operational conditions, and limitations of each device will be discussed. An evaluation of each category of equipment will be based on the overall performance standard.

Finally, a list of some major manufacturers of commercially available equipment, presently used worldwide for oil/water separation, will be compiled.

APPROACH

This project will identify, organize, and interpret technical and commercial literature resources on oil/water separation.

The first effort will be a description of the various states in which oil can co-exist with water after intimate contact of both liquids. Each of the states will be characterized in operational terms, as well as in the physical-chemical sense. Next, the process streams to be considered—oily wastewaters generated onboard ship, oil in process water, and formation water from crude oil production—will be characterized based on oil/water system states. Other parameters to be considered for an efficient separation will be outlined.

The second phase will be devoted to a review of the state-of-the-art of separation devices and processes. A distinction will be made between device performance and the performance of a chain of several devices or a process. Since the performance standard of each device is of utmost importance, the review of a device will be reported using the following format:

a) title of report;
b) report number and date of report;
c) author(s);
d) manufacturer of equipment;
e) design features;
f) characteristics of wastewater on which device was tested;
g) method(s) of analysis;
h) results (performance of standard based on published data);
i) approximate purchase price of equipment (if specified); and
j) critical comments.

2

The overall effectiveness of each class of devices for separation of oil/ water system states will be noted.

Finally, a list of manufacturers for each equipment category will be compiled. Material to be reviewed is generated through searches in available commercial literature and unpublished reports of industries and laboratories involved in the manufacture or testing of equipment and new techniques. Since existing literature is vast, the search and review process will focus primarily on utility, rather than exhaustiveness.

SECTION 2

CONCLUSIONS

This report is a review of the state-of-the-art for oil/water separating devices and processes. Techniques proposed as feasible but not yet evaluated as candidates for oil/water separation are discussed also. Discussion does not include coagulation-flocculation processes with chemical addition, nor is the list of devices exhaustive.

The problems associated with the removal of oil from water are complex; to meet effluent guidelines or discharge limits, many oil/water treatment facilities must be upgraded. Before a choice of separating equipment can be made, the specific nature of the oil/water separation problem has to be examined thoroughly. Sources of oily wastewaters are diverse; oily wastewaters produced by different processes have characteristics that differ from each other depending on the type of oil(s), oil(s) and suspended-solids concentrations, physical and chemical properties of the aqueous phase, the process originating the oily wastes, salinity, temperature, etc. Moreover, the characteristics of oily wastewaters may change with time. The problem is complicated further by the different states in which oil can exist in water. The thermodynamic states in which oil can exist in water have not been identified completely; only the major states have been described. These states can co-exist in wastewater depending on oil type, degree of mixing of the oil and water phases, concentration of surfactants, and other factors. Also, it is difficult to estimate oil concentrations in given oily wastewaters, because of inadequate analytical methods. Concentrations of states depend on the chemical interactions between oil and water, number of days of equilibration, and the dissolution processes (physical, bacterial, or chemical oxidation) occurring during the equilibration period.

Each state has a certain degree of difficulty associated with its removal. There are many devices available commercially capable of removing one or a few states, but a single device capable of separating all states is still lacking. With progress in membrane technology, reverse osmosis and ultrafiltration may qualify eventually as the best technologies available for separating oil/water mixtures. For economic reasons, carbon adsorption should continue to be used in polishing states. The potential and limitations of devices and processes are presented in Table 1.

The degree of difficulty of separating oil from wastewaters depends largely on the number of states present. Because of the inability of devices to effectively separate several states, combination of separation techniques into process trains is necessary to produce effluents that will meet discharge standards. A modern oil wastewater treatment system may include an API gravity separator and dissolved air flotation for removing free oil,

4

TABLE 1. POTENTIAL OF SEPARATION TECHNIQUES TO SEPARATE VARIOUS OIL/WATER SYSTEM STATES

Technique	Free oil	Oil-coated solids Settleable	Oil-coated solids Neutrally buoyant	Unstabilized dispersions Primary	Unstabilized dispersions Secondary	Stabilized dispersions Chemically	Stabilized dispersions Surface charge	Solubilized oil	Molecularly dissolved oil
A. Gravity									
Differential									
API	XXX *	XX		X					
Hydrogard	XXX	XX		X					
Circular	XXX	XX		X					
PPI	XXX	XX		XX					
CPI	XXX	XX		XX	X				
Fram-Akers	XXX	XXX	XXX	XXX	XX				
Curved-plate finger	XXX	XXX	XX	XX	X				
Gravi-Pak	XXX	XXX		XXX					
Centrifuges	XXX	XXX		XXX					
Hydrocyclones	XX	XXX							
Vortex	XX	XX							
Dispersed air flotation	XXX	XXX	X	XX					
Dissolved air flotation	XXX	XXX	XX	XXX	XX				
Vacuum desorption	XXX	XXX	XX	XXX	XX				
Electrochemical			X	XX	XX		XXX		
B. Filtration									
Granular media		XXX	XXX	XXX	XX	X	X		
Multimedia		XXX	XXX	XXX	XXX	XX	XX		
C. Coalescence/ Filtration									
Fibrous media	XXX			XXX	XXX				
Centrifuge	XXX			XXX	XXX				
Bimetallic					XX		XXX		

*X, poor separation; XX, average separation; XXX, excellent separation.

5

TABLE 1. POTENTIAL OF SEPARATION TECHNIQUES TO SEPARATE VARIOUS OIL/WATER SYSTEM STATES (cont.)

Technique	Free oil	Oil-coated solids Settle-able	Neutrally buoyant	Unstabilized dispersions Primary	Secondary	Stabilized dispersions Chemically	Surface charge	Solubilized oil	Molecularly dissolved oil
D. Membrane									
Electro-dialysis	XX *			XX	XX	XX	XX	X	X
Reverse osmosis	XXX			XXX	XXX	XXX	XXX	XXX	XXX
Ultrafiltration	XXX			XXX	XXX	XXX	XXX	XXX	XX
E. Adsorption									
Carbon			XXX		XXX	XXX	XXX	XXX	XXX
F. Electric & Magnetic									
Electrophoretic					X		XX		
Magnetic					XX				
G. Thermal				XX	X				
H. Coanda Effect	X								
I. Viscosity-Actuated	X								
J. Chromatography								XXX	XXX
K. Sonic & Ultrasonic				X	X	X			

*X, poor separation; XX, average separation; XXX, excellent separation.

6

oil-coated suspended solids, and unemulsified primary dispersions; a co-alescer equipped with a prefilter for removing neutrally buoyant, oil-coated solids and remaining unemulsified primary and secondary dispersions; reverse osmosis for removing emulsified, solubilized, and dissolved oil; and carbon adsorption for removing the last traces of dissolved oil. A combination of other separation methods can be used; however, the general trend is gross separation followed by finer separation and, finally, a polishing state. This trend should prove to be most economical; desired effluent quality can be achieved, the life of the polishing stage is extended, and throughput is reasonable. Therefore, utilization of several separation techniques is an efficient means of separating oil/water mixtures.

An attempt to review patent literature was unsuccessful, because of the limited information usually available in patents and absence of performance data.

It is hoped the information developed in this report will be useful to both manufacturers and users of oil/water separating equipment.

SECTION 3

RECOMMENDATIONS

1. The thermodynamic states in which oil can co-exist with water are not
   defined completely. Identification of oil/water system states present
   in a given wastewater is necessary to a good choice of separating
   devices.

2. Dissolution rates of a variety of oils, petroleum products, and other
   toxic organic pollutants are in need of measurement.

3. Until recently, it was thought that the concentration of dissolved oil
   present in effluents could not be higher than the solubility of the oil.
   The phenomenon of solubilization of oil, in the presence of surface-
   active agents and dissolved organic matter, increases oil concentrations
   considerably. Therefore, removal of dissolved oil is necessary if
   effluents are to meet discharge limits. Solubilization of oil should
   be investigated.

4. Estimating oil content with on-line oil/water monitors, turbidity measurements, visual observation, and other dubious analytical techniques
   should be avoided. Oil/water monitors and turbidity meters are highly
   variable. Since regulations are aimed at the total oil content of
   effluents, total organic carbon analysis should be preferred over
   extraction-gravimetric or extraction-infrared-spectrophotometric techniques for measuring oil content of oil/distilled water samples.

5. The efficiencies of different organic solvents--heptane, hexane, chloroform, carbon tetrachloride, petroleum ether, pentane, and methylene
   chloride--commonly used in extracting oil for analysis, must be investigated. Efficiencies of solvents for different hydrocarbon groups
   (paraffins, aromatics, etc.) merit investigation. Depending on the
   solvent and the number of extractions, results of oil concentrations in
   effluents can be in great error.

6. Since oil dispersions are formed through turbulent mixing during pumping
   operations, the efficiency of separation can be enhanced by gravity flow
   or use of low-shear pumps having limited emulsification tendencies.

7. A method to characterize oily wastewaters in terms of separation
   requirements is needed.

8. For any oily-waste problem, segregation of wastes containing detergents,
   proper water management techniques, maintenance of devices in good

operating condition, and adequate operator training are useful.

9. Presently, there is no format for evaluating the performance of oil/water separation devices. Oil/water mixtures used in test evaluations should be characteristic of the oily wastewaters that the equipment will treat upon installation. Tests using oil/water emulsions formed by passage through a centrifugal pump do not demonstrate equipment capability to separate other emulsions without data on comparative emulsion stability. Factors that affect the efficiency of the separation process should be varied systematically.

10. Many performance claims are substantiated with limited test results, using inexact analytical methods. Performance data are not stated, often because data are considered proprietary. Often, devices have not been tested adequately. Therefore, evaluation can be made only by comparing the principles of separation, instead of design variations and/or special design features.

11. For comparison of promising techniques and adequate evaluation of existing technology, a test facility similar to OHMSETT is needed.

SECTION 4

SYSTEM CHARACTERIZATION

OIL/WATER SYSTEMS

Before a separation device or process can be selected, there is need for an understanding of the type of oily wastewater to be treated. As such, a characterization of oil/water systems is necessary. In this discussion, "oil" will be used in a generic sense to refer to the non-aqueous phase and "water" will refer to the aqueous phase.

After intimate contact of oil and water, oil can contaminate the water by existing in the aqueous phase in various forms. These states have already been identified and reported in the literature as free oil, dispersed oil, chemically emulsified oil, molecularly dissolved and solubilized oil, and oil-coated suspended solids.

FREE OIL

When a mixture of oil and water is left undisturbed for a short time, a continuous layer of oil forms at the surface of the aqueous phase if the oil is less dense than water. Separation of the mixture into two separate layers is due to the action of buoyant forces on the large oil masses initially present in the water body. The oil in the top layer has the essential physical and chemical properties of the source (parent) oil, unless it has been modified by extrusion or reaction with chemicals present in the aqueous environment. Modification may be due, also, to the action of any or all of the following mechanisms: evaporation of the volatile components, atmospheric oxidation, microbial activity, and dissolution of soluble fractions of the oil. These processes occur if there is prolonged contact of the liquids, e.g. ballast and bilge waters retained onboard vessels for several days or weeks.

DISPERSED OIL (EMULSIONS)

Due to turbulent mixing, oil droplets may be dispersed in the aqueous phase to form an oil-in-water emulsion, depending on phase volume ratios and other factors. The particle size of the dispersed oil in an emulsion is important in characterizing the type of dispersion. Depending on the intensity of mixing, primary or secondary dispersions result. Both dispersions usually account for only a very small volume fraction of oil, in the order of 50 to 1,000 ppm.

Primary dispersions are formed from macroscopic oil droplets that range in diameter from 1,000 to 10,000 Å and remain in suspension due to Brownian motion. These droplets are generally unstable thermodynamically and agglomerate or coalesce into larger droplets, if allowed to remain undisturbed for periods of approximately 24 hours. Primary dispersions are produced by low shear pumps, e.g. diaphragm and vane pumps, as well as low-speed centrifugal pumps.

Secondary dispersions are formed from very fine, microscopic oil droplets that have mean diameters between 50 and 600 Å and do not separate from water if left undisturbed for a very long time; they are stable thermodynamically. Highly turbulent flow conditions are favorable to the formation of secondary dispersions.

Interfacial tension is an effective stabilization mechanism for dispersions. Additional stability of dispersions arises if electrical charges are present on the surfaces of oil droplets. A detailed discussion on this electrokinetic phenomenon can be found in the literature (Kruyt, 1952; Overbeek, 1952; Adamson, 1967). A double layer of charges is formed at the oil/water interface of each droplet, and coalescence of adjacent droplets is prevented by mutual repulsion. The potential difference in the diffuse double layer is called the zeta potential. Stable emulsions exhibit zeta potentials in excess of 25 mV (Churchill and Kaufman, 1973; Orr and Kang, 1974). Measurement of this potential is a useful tool in estimating the stability of emulsions (Orr and Kang, 1974).

CHEMICALLY STABILIZED DISPERSIONS

The presence of surfactants favors formation of chemically stabilized dispersions. These have the same particle sizes as the primary and secondary dispersions discussed above. The oil droplets have additional stability because of the presence of a third component in either the oily or the aqueous phase. The third component is variously referred to as a surfactant, surface-active agent, detergent, soap, stabilizing agent, emulsifier, etc. Small concentrations of this agent are enough to chemically stabilize oil droplets. Extensive literature is available on surfactants and their effects on the stability of emulsions (Jefferson and Boulavare, 1973; Churchill and Kaufman, 1973; Gloyna and Ford, 1974). The chemical nature of the surfactant is important. A theory has been advanced for surfactant modification of an oil/water interface. It states that surfactants are molecules composed of lipophilic and hydrophilic end groups that orient themselves in an emulsion such that their lipophilic ends project into the non-aqueous phase while their hydrophilic ends are anchored in the aqueous phase. A protective "film" is formed around each droplet, as a result of surface interaction. Reduction in interfacial tension leads to a low free energy, which is unfavorable to coalescence of the oil droplets.

MOLECULARLY DISSOLVED OIL

Generally, hydrocarbons exhibit limited solubilities in water, with aromatic hydrocarbons somewhat more soluble than aliphatic hydrocarbons

11

(McAuliffe, 1969a,b). Molecularly dissolved oil is oil that is in true chemical solution in the aqueous phase. Dissolved oil is generally classified as submicroscopic oil droplets, below 50-Å diameter. Because of limited solubility of oils in water, the concentration of molecularly dissolved oil is probably less than 20 ppm. However, after prolonged equilibration, oil concentrations can be higher than 200 ppm. Dissolution of petroleum-derived products has been studied extensively, but is not completely understood (McAuliffe, 1969a; Boehm and Quinn, 1974; Lysyj and Russell, 1974). One reason for the inadequacy of knowledge in this subject is the lack of technology for measuring soluble oil without interference from emulsion droplets. Lai and Adams (1974) developed a method for determining the molecular solubility of Navy oils in water, using an osmometric device.

SOLUBILIZED OIL

Studies indicate that, in the presence of dissolved organic matter (DOM) in the aqueous phase, the solubility of oils increases, particularly oils containing large fractions of aliphatic hydrocarbons (Boehm, 1973; Boehm and Quinn, 1974). Acceleration of organics transfer into the aquous phase is due to chemical modification of water-insoluble petroleum fractions. The presence of surface-active agents in petroleum products can cause solubilization, also. Solubilized oil droplets are less than 0.5 μ in size. Solubilization of hydrocarbons in seawater may not be appreciable if the DOM concentration is so low that the concentration of dissolved surfactants does not exceed the critical micelle concentration (Elworthy et al., 1968).

OIL-COATED SUSPENDED SOLIDS

Solids suspended in the aqueous phase become coated with oil. These solids have a wide range of origins, densities, compositions, and sizes (Finger and Tabakin, 1973; Freestone and Tabakin, 1975). These solids are mainly clays, silica, drill muds, corrosion products, asphaltenes, heavy metals or alkaline-earth salts, and the fine sediments that are abundant in natural waters and oil field brine formation water. Finely divided solids play a major role in crude oil emulsion stabilization. Solids that are neutrally buoyant require special treatment before they can be separated effectively. Oil adsorbed on the surfaces of solids enhances solubilization.

12

SECTION 5

CHARACTERIZATION OF OILY WASTEWATERS

Since this review focuses primarily on technology available for separating oily wastewaters from ships and crude oil production operations, a brief characterization of these wastewaters in parallel with the characterization of oil/water systems follows.

Oily wastewaters generated onboard ships and vessels are ballast water, tank cleaning water, and bilge water.

BALLAST WATER

After discharging fuel oil cargo, a ship pumps water or seawater into storage tanks to maintain stability. This water may contain large amounts of silt or fine solids if picked up in a river or estuary, or offshore from a large seaward river flow. Oil that adheres to tank walls mixes with the water as a result of ship motion. During deballasting operations, the oily wastewater is pumped out, usually by a high-speed centrifugal or reciprocating pump, in order to minimize turnaround time. The phase-forming effects of various pumps on mixtures of oil and water have been reviewed (Shackleton et al., 1960; Fruman and Sundaram, 1974). Many factors affect the dispersion of oil/water mixtures as they pass through pumps and piping (Shackleton et al., 1960):

a) excessive velocities and accelerations;
b) restricted ducts;
c) rapid changes in fluid direction; and
d) varying speeds and discharge pressures.

It is likely that deballasted water contains all the oil/water systems discussed in Section 4, depending on the following factors:

a) type of fuel cargo;
b) characteristics of water used as ballast water;
c) duration of voyage between ballasting and deballasting operations; and
d) the emulsification characteristics of the pump used in deballasting.

Ballast water from cargo tanks usually contains oily residues from prior loads. Occasionally, washwater from tank cleaning is added to ballast water.

13

TANK-CLEANING WATER

Before a change in fuel cargo is made, cargo tanks are washed. Oily
wastewater generated by tank cleaning is similar to ballast water, except
detergent cleaning of cargo tanks may be necessary. Cleaning with detergents leads to formation of chemically emulsified oil. The amount of oil
that clings to tank walls may be up to 1% of the total cargo, depending on
the viscosity of the oil. This portion of the load ends up in ballast and
tank-cleaning waters. Dirt and scale are produced by tank cleaning, also.

BILGE WATER

Bilge water comprises leakages of lubricating oil, fuel oils, and hydraulic fluids, and water resulting from drains and drippings in the engine
room. It contains solids and rust scale, also. Oils present in bilge water
contain many additives. Bilge water must be pumped out of the ship, and
chemically emulsified oil will be the dominant of the two types of emulsions discussed previously. Becuase of the complexity of bilge waters,
there is, as yet, no meaningful characterization scheme (Budininkas and
Remus, 1974). In undiluted bilge water, the ratio of oil-to-water is higher
than in ballast water. Therefore, multiple emulsions are probably present.
The rate at which a ship generates bilge depends on the age, condition, and
maintenance history.

OIL-FIELD PRODUCTION WATER

There is increasing interest in development of offshore oil production
facilities. During crude oil exploration, drill cuttings and mud chemicals
are the main pollutants. In the production phase, the wastewater generated
is oily brine formation water (production water). The composition of formation water differs from well to well. However, these wastewaters are characterized by a high content of dissolved and suspended solids. Therefore,
the potential for formation of oil-coated solids and stable emulsions is
high.

Crude oils are complex mixtures; they differ in characteristics,
according to geologic age, chemical constitution, and associated impurities.
They contain many natural emulsifiers, usually naphthenic and other organic
acids, resinous substances, and asphaltenes (Reisberg and Doscher, 1956).
Formation brines for different wells have different compositions (USEPA,
1975). Consequently, emulsions resulting from crude oil production are
stabilized by a variety of mechanisms, depending on origin.

Discharge pressures during crude oil production are usually high, and
entrainment of fine gas bubbles in the oil/water mixture is likely to occur.

SUMMARY

The various states in which oil and water can co-exist have been discussed. Oily wastewaters from vessels and crude oil production have been
characterized crudely. Technology available for the separation of these
oily wastewaters will be reviewed.

14

In addition to the oil/water system states already presented, other parameters influence the performance of a separation device or process:

a) oil concentration of the influent stream;
b) flow rate;
c) physio-chemical properties of the wastewater, including
   1) temperature,
   2) pH,
   3) salinity,
   4) ionic strength, and
   5) dielectric constant;
d) density ratio of the oily and aqueous phases; and
e) mechanical motions during separation.

SECTION 6

DEVICES AND PROCESSES

Available methods for separating oil/water mixtures include: physical, chemical, mechanical, electrical, magnetic, and thermal treatments, and combinations of these. Because manufacturers' trade names are often misleading, devices are classified according to the primary mechanism which induces separation in wastewaters. The basic principle of each group of devices is stated. Variations in devices and processes, including the different modes of operation, are specified. Pertinent literature on a device, particularly literature on text evaluation of equipment, is summarized and reviewed critically.

Since the performance standard for each class of devices is of utmost importance, the workability of each group relative to what is known about oil/water system states is discussed. The specific oil/water system(s) which each group of devices (if adequately designed and operated) is capable of treating is noted.

Applicability of devices relative to some additional constraints is stated. These include: limiting space requirements, low weight, and sensitivity to motion during processing. These are imposed by shipboard or offshore platform operations, but are not necessarily important for shoreside facilities. Finally, it should be noted that this survey does not purport to include all devices presently available.

TECHNOLOGY

Commercial and experimental oil/water separation devices are listed below. Devices operating on principles proposed as feasible but which are, as yet, in the developmental stage are included.

Gravity Differential Separation

    API Oil/Water Separators
    Circular Separators
    Plate Separators
        Shell parallel-plate interceptors (PPI)
        Shell corrugated-plate interceptors (CPI)
    Curved-Plate Finger Separators
    Rotational Separation
        Centrifuges
        Hydrocyclones
        Vortex flow

16

Gas Flotation
  Dispersed air
  Dissolved air
  Vacuum desorption
  Electrochemical

Filtration

Layer Filtration
  Granular media .
  Multimedia
Membrane
  Electrodialysis
  Reverse osmosis
  Ultrafiltration

Coalescence/Filtration

Fibrous-Media
Membrane
Centrifuge
Bimetallic
Granular-Media
Other Porous Materials

Adsorption and Absorption

Electric and Magnetic Separation

Electrophoretic
Magnetic

Thermal Separation

Heating
Evaporation and Distillation
Freezing and Crystallization

Sonic and Ultrasonic Separation

Coanda-Effect Separation

Viscosity-Actuated Phase Separation

Chromatographic Separation

Gravity Differential Separation

Gravity differential separation is the oldest and most common method for separating oil/water mixtures. It is usually the first step in the treatment of oily wastewaters and provides coarse separation of oil and water. In

17

general, oil/water mixtures will separate naturally into two distinct layers of oil and water, if allowed to stand undisturbed for a sufficient period of time. Ease of separation depends on the magnitude of the difference in densities of the two immiscible liquids; the basic principle governing this technique is Stokes's Law, which is applicable to the rate of rise of oil globules in water.

$$v = \frac{gD^2(\delta_\omega - \delta_o)}{18\mu}$$

where v = rate of rise of an oil globule

   g = acceleration due to gravity

   D = diameter of an oil globule

   δ_ω, δ_o = densities of the aqueous phase and oil, respectively

   μ = absolute viscosity of the aqueous phase

Stokes's Law applies to solids suspended in water (oil-coated), also. From this equation, oil globules and/or suspended particles will rise to the surface or fall to the bottom, depending on the sign of the density differential. The difference in densities between most contaminant oils and water is usually small, and the viscosity of the aqueous phase is temperature-dependent but is essentially constant. Therefore, the rate of rise of an oil globule is dependent to a large extent on the particle size. Hence, for an appreciable separation to occur, within reasonable residence times, the oil droplets and suspended solids must be large. As oil globules rise to the surface, collisions occur, coalescence takes place, and a floating oil film forms at the surface. Coalesced oil is subsequently skimmed off.

Gravity separation is inefficient when the density difference is small, viscosity of the aqueous phase is low, and oil droplets are small. As particle size becomes smaller, residence times and space requirements increase. Because of these limitations, gravity separation methods are used only to separate free oil, primary dispersions, and large oil-coated solids. Devices operating on the gravity principle will not separate dissolved oil or emulsions (API, 1969). Neutrally buoyant solids, coated with oil, are not separated. If gravity separation is used in conjunction with chemical addition, stable emulsions can be broken and separated.

The most economical state-of-the-art methods in oil/water separation are of the gravity type. Devices can handle large flow rates, have low power requirements, and need minimum operator attention; but processes are slow, necessitating large equipment. Gravity separation is basic to almost all oil/water separators. Several methods have been devised for accelerating the process. These include provisions for heating the influent to reduce the viscosity of the aqueous phase, extended plate surfaces to increase the horizontal distance traveled by oil globules, rotational forces instead of gravitational force, and air flotation. In attempts to increase oil/water separation efficiency, there have been modifications of existing designs. As a result, devices in this category are the most abundant. The slight variations and modifications in designs have already been reviewed excellently by Harris (1973). Of major concern are the improvement of the hydraulic

18

characteristics of the devices and the reduction of turbulence in separators. Almost all gravity-type separators produce effluents that must be treated further, in subsequent separating devices. However, they are reliable, simple, and inexpensive to operate, and serve to attentuate fluctuations in flow and oil concentration in lieu of more sophisticated oil/water separators.

API Oil/Water Separators--The design of gravity-type separators has been studied extensively by several investigators and particularly by the American Petroleum Institute (Ingersoll, 1951; Rohlich, 1951; University of Wisconsin, 1949, 1950, 1951). As a result of these efforts, the API has set forth design recommendations for oil/water separators in the Manual on Disposal of Refinery Wastes: Volume on Liquid Wastes (API, 1969). Construction details of API separators are found in Chapter 6 of the manual. Important design considerations are minimum horizontal area, minimum vertical cross-sectional area, and minimum depth-to-width ratio of 0.3-0.5. The API design is based on Stokes's Law and hydraulic overflow rates. An oil-droplet rise rate of 0.2 ft/min, with a forward wastewater flow of 3.00 ft/min, is used. Detention time is about one-half hour. Separators are designed to remove non-emulsified oil particles of 130-150 μ and larger for oils having typical specific gravity. Design nomographs are presented in the manual, with corrections for turbulence, short-circuiting, and wastewater temperature. API separators are usually rectangular in shape and multichanneled; expansion is possible, and single channels can be cleaned without interrupting operation. The API oil/water separator consists of inlet and outlet sections, a pre-treatment stage, separating stages, baffles, skimming devices, and flight scrapers. Some separators are equipped with covers or floating roofs. In operation, oily wastewater enters the separator at the inlet, flow is slowed down, and turbulence is minimized by the inlet structure and baffles. Oil globules larger than 150 μ rise to the surface and settleable solids (oil-coated and non-oil-coated) sink to the bottom. Provision is made for skimming the oil and removing the sludge. A schematic diagram of an AFI oil/water separator is given in Figure 1.

Hydrogard separators are prepackaged oil/water separator units, manufactured by Inland Environmental Corporation. These separators are designed according to API guidelines. Units with flow rates up to 210 gpm are available. Cleaning and maintenance are carried out easily. Inland Environmental Corporation claims that effluents from these separators can contain as little as 5 ppm of oil.

Circular Separators--Oil/water separators designed according to the conventional arrangement of a circular clarifier are used in some oil refineries with satisfactory results, but a rational design procedure for circular separators has not been developed. An advantage of circular units is the ease of installing oil-skimming and sludge-scraping devices. The capacity of these devices can be varied by adjusting the height of the oil skimmer. Oily wastewater is fed through a central inlet; effluent outlets are located in the peripheral wall. Circular units are more compact than API separators.

Plate Separators--Concern over the large space requirements of API oil/water separators led to studies on methods of reducing equipment size without decreasing oil-removal efficiency. Different methods were used to reduce

19

SEPARATOR CHANNEL

DIFFUSION DEVICE
(VERTICAL-SLOT BAFFLE)

FLIGHT SCRAPER
CHAIN SPROCKET

ROTATABLE OIL-
SKIMMING PIPE

OIL-RETENTION
BAFFLE

GATEWAY PIER

EFFLUENT
WEIR AND
WALL

WOOD FLIGHTS

FLIGHT
SCRAPER
CHAIN

WATER
LEVEL

FLOW

FOREBAY

SLOT FOR
CHANNEL GATE

SLUDGE-COLLECTING HOPPER
DISCHARGE WITH LEAD PIPE

EFFLUENT FLUME

EFFLUENT SEWER

SLUDGE-COLLECTING
HOPPER

SLUDGE PUMP
SUCTION PIPE

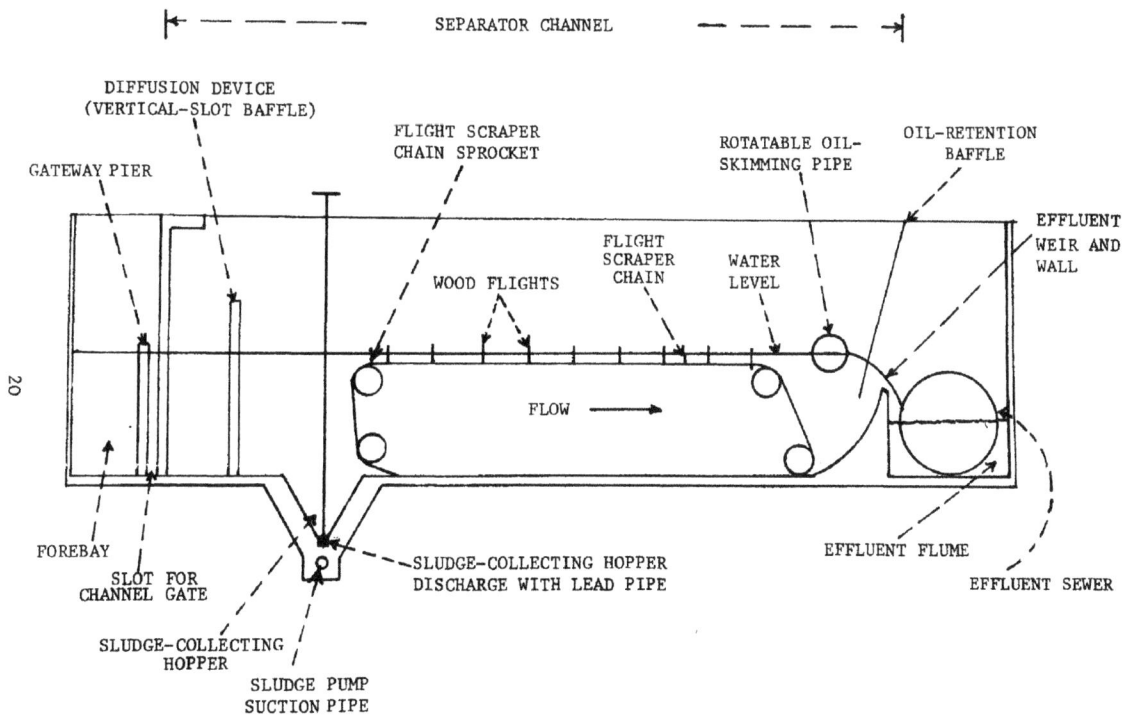

Figure 1. API Oil/Water Separator

settling length, because the time required for oil particles to rise to the surface depends on the depth of the separator. Flat plates, plate packs, convoluted plates, perforated conical plates, and perforated plates of other geometry have been used to subdivide the settling chamber into a number of sections. Plates increase the surface area and reduce the maximum rise height of oil globules. It is observed that coalescence of oil globules occurs on these plates, also, Therefore, the maximum distance oil droplets have to travel, before coalescence occurs, is dependent on plate spacing instead of depth as in the API design. To improve coalescence, plates are manufactured from oleophilic materials and inclined at an angle to the incoming flow. As oil globules rise to the surface, they coalesce on the underside of the plates, creep up plate surfaces and break loose as large particles that rise rapidly to the top. Because of these design modifications, plate separators are approximately one-fifth to one-half the size of API separators. Oil skimming and sludge removal are easier; the main problem with these units is plugging of the spaces between plates with solids, biological growth, or highly viscous oils. Several types of plate separators are available commercially.

Shell parallel-plate interceptor. The Shell parallel-plate interceptor (PPI) oil/water separator has parallel plates spaced 100 mm (approximately 4 inches) apart. Two such systems are available. One system consists of one or more sets of plates inclined at an angle of 45° to the long axis of the separator. The other system consists of one set of plates parallel to the long axis and inclined at an angle of 45° to the horizontal. The spacing between the plates can be varied. Because of the inclination, the effective surface area for coalescence is increased and the net path oil globules travel before reaching the surface is decreased (Kirby, 1964). These added features make the Shell PPI oil/water separator capable of separating oil droplets of 60 μ in diameter or larger. In spite of improvement in performance, stable emulsions and dissolved oil cannot be separated in these devices.

Shell corrugated-plate interceptor (CPI). An improvement on the Shell PPI oil/water separator design is the Shell CPI separator. It features plates arranged at an angle of 45° to the horizontal in the direction of wastewater flow, similar to the Shell PPI unit; the major difference is that the plates are corrugated and the spacing between plates is smaller, only approximately 20 to 40 mm. Plates are made of fiber glass-reinforced polyester. Because of closer spacing, CPI units are more compact than PPI units and oil-removal efficiency is greater. Reduction in space requirement can be as high as two-thirds, but plugging from solids is a major problem. Newer designs feature accesses for easy cleaning. Schematic diagrams of the Shell PPI and CPI are given in Figures 2 and 3, respectively.

The Fram Corporation manufactures an oil/water separating system featuring a combination of two separation processes. The separator has three stages: the first stage contains two preconditioners (filter-cartridge type, having 75-μ pore openings) for suspended-solids removal; the second stage utilizes parallel-plate-type gravity separation; and the third stage contains a cartridge-type coalescer. Because of the presence of a cartridge-type coalescer, this system is capable of breaking and separating emulsions. Compact design makes the system suitable for use on board ship. Oil-removal

VENT AND OIL
OVERFLOW PIPE

OVERFLOW PIPE FOR
TREATED WATER

TREATED
WATER

TRASH
CONTAINER

SCREEN

OIL LAYER

PACKS OF PARALLEL
INCLINED PLATES

SLUDGE SUMP

SUCTION HOSE
FOR SLUDGE

SAND SUMP

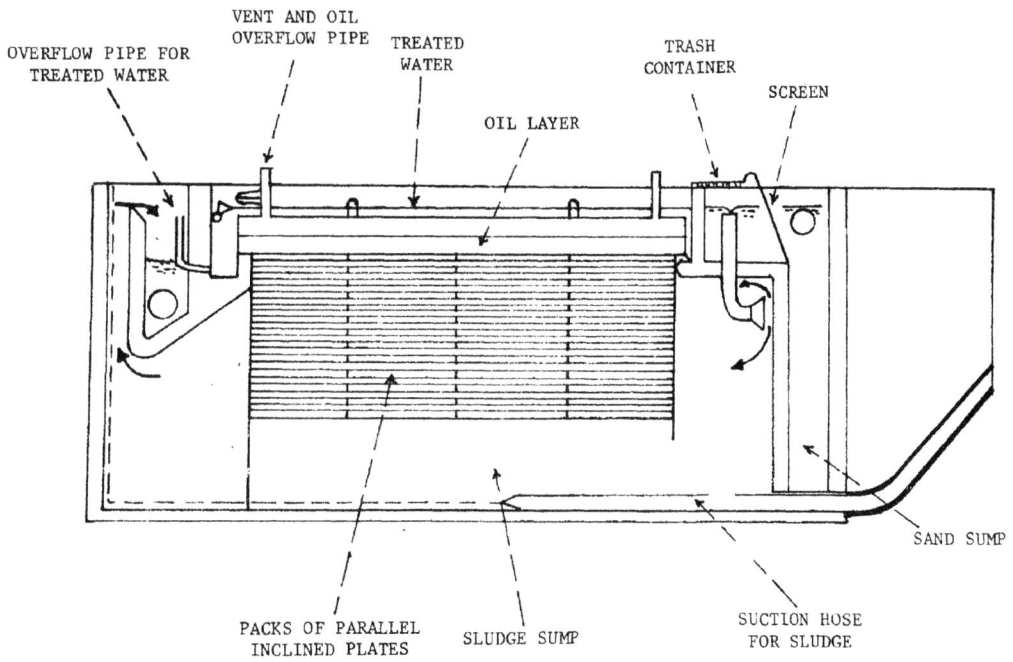

Figure 2. Shell Parallel-Plate Interceptor

ADJUSTABLE WEIR

OIL SKIMMER

OIL LAYER

OIL GLOBULES

INLET

OUTLET

SEDIMENT TRAP

TREATED WATER OUTLET CHANNEL

PACKS OF CORRUGATED PARALLEL PLATES

SLUDGE PIT

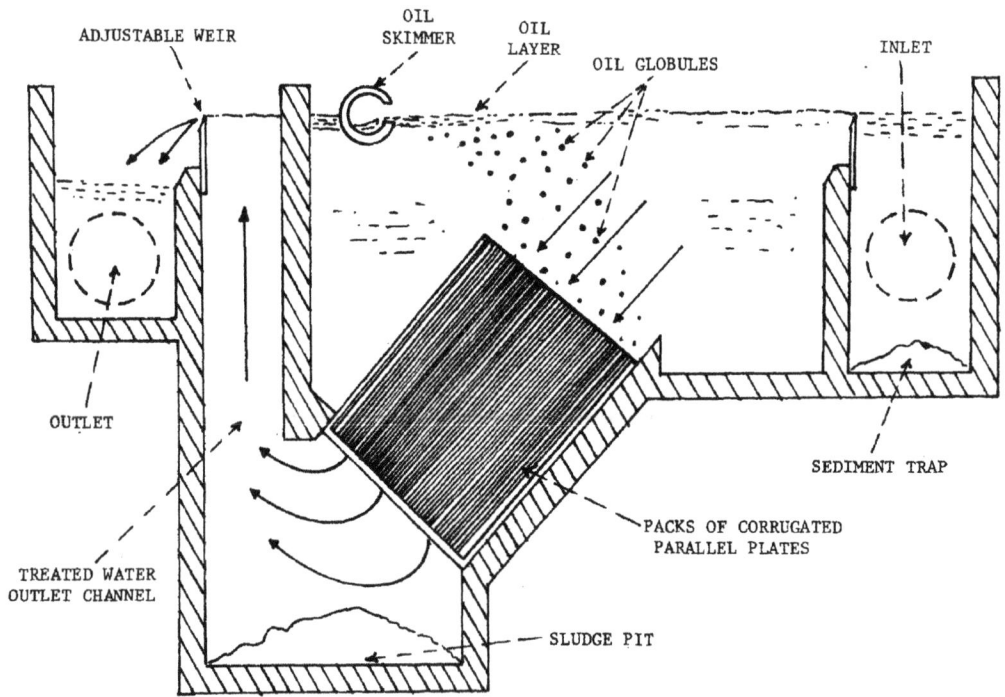

Figure 3. Shell Corrugated-Plate Interceptor

efficiency is reasonable, but effluents require some further treatment before discharge. Media plugging and low liquid flow rates are disadvantages. System backwashing, when head loss reaches a specified level, is automatic.

Curved-Plate Finger Separators--The basis for the design of the curved-plate finger separator is accelerated gravity settling of oil from oily wastewaters. This separation technique is a combination of gas flotation and parallel plate-type gravity separation. Incoming wastewater feed is first mixed with air, as in dispersed gas flotation; the separation of oil and water takes place between curved steel plates. The plates are inclined horizontally and arranged in the direction of flow. Oil films form at the undersides of the plates, rise gradually toward the upper ends of the plates, and leave as "fingers" at the plate tips. Oil that collects at the surface is removed by an oil-skimming device. Because of the gas flotation characteristics of this device, small oil globules can be separated. Space requirements are less than for API oil/water separators, for the same throughput.

The Gravi-Pak oil/water separator is manufactured by Keene Corporation. Units are multistaged, and consist of a primary separation chamber of the parallel-plate type and a secondary separation stage in which natural gravity settling occurs. Devices are suitable for gross separation of oil and water and are more compact than the API design, but larger than Fram-Akers units. Manufacturers claim effluents from these units can contain less than 30 ppm of oil, with wastewater having up to 20,000 ppm of oil.

Design--Stokes's Law is the fundamental principle governing design of gravity-type oil/water separators. Design considerations are flow rate, rise rate of oil globules, turbulence correction factors, type and concentration of oil, characteristics of wastewater, and geometry of basin.

Performance--Gravity-type oil/water separators are used primarily to remove free oil, large oil globules (unstable primary dispersions), and oil-and/or non-oil-coated solids in suspension. Stable emulsions (surface- or chemically stabilized), solubilized oil, and dissolved oil are not separated by devices operating on the gravity differential principle. Devices can handle varying influent oil concentration and are normally used for gross separation. Effluents from these devices usually require some further treatment before discharge. Factors affecting oil-removal efficiency are flow rate, oil particle size, density of oil, characteristics of wastewater, temperature, and separator design. For good separation, it is essential that feed velocity distribution is as uniform as possible at the inlet section of the device.

The API oil/water separator is an effective and versatile device for removing oil and suspended solids. Because of design limitations, API separators are only effective in removing oil globules having a lower limit of 130 μ in diameter. Neutrally buoyant particles may pass out with the effluent. Beychok (1973) has summarized the available performance data on API separators. His data are presented in Table 2. Data indicate that oil content of effluents can be as high as 120 ppm, when the oil content of influents is small. Operation of devices at flow rates grossly below design

24

rates yields lower efficiencies. In experiments with a cylindrical-type separator having a residence time of about 20 minutes, at a flow rate of 10 gpm, Finger and Tabakin (1973) report that more than 80% of the oil was removed from oily wastewaters containing up to 4% oil. The performance data of several gravity-type separators, published by Gloyna and Ford (1974), are presented in Table 3. Oil-removal efficiencies, for refinery wastes, range from 50 to 90%. Data indicate that oil-removal efficiencies in parallel-plate separators may be higher than achievable in API separators. A comparison of results of API and PPI separators by Kirby (1964) indicates reductions in oil content of up to 67% more in the PPI than in the API. Data presented by Brunsmann et al. (1962) substantiate the belief that PPI separators achieve higher oil removal than comparable API separators. Harris (1973) presents estimated effluent quality from primary oil/water separation processes, as shown in Table 4. The oil content of effluents from devices operating on the gravity differential principle can be much higher. Effluents containing more than 500 ppm of oil should be expected, if the influent contains high concentrations of emulsified and dissolved oil. Average oil removal of 25 to 65% should be expected; oil-removal efficiency can be increased to more than 80%, if the process is used in conjunction with chemical addition. Suspended-solids (oil-coated and/or non-oil-coated) removal of up to 65% can be accomplished. Gravity-type separators will continue to be basic to treatment of oily wastes; and operation of devices, at design flow rates by trained personnel, will yield reasonable separation.

TABLE 2. OIL REMOVAL IN API SEPARATORS[*]

| Oil content (ppm) | | % Removal | Shape |
Influent	Effluent		
-	20-70	-	Rectangular
-	20	-	"
-	80-115	-	"
-	75	-	"
50-100	20-40	60	"
90-98	40-44	55	"
42	20	52	"
108	20	54	Circular

TABLE 3. OIL AND SUSPENDED-SOLIDS REMOVAL IN GRAVITY-TYPE SEPARATORS[*]

Oil content (ppm)		% Oil removal	% Suspended-solids removal	Type
Influent	Effluent			
300	40	87	-	PPI
220	49	78	-	API
108	20	82	-	circular
108	50	54	-	"
98	44	55	-	API
100	40	60	-	"
42	20	52	-	"
2000	746	63	33	"
1250	170	87	68	"
1400	270	81	35	"

[*] Gloyna and Ford (1974).

TABLE 4. ESTIMATED EFFLUENT QUALITY FROM PRIMARY OIL/WATER SEPARATION PROCESSES[*]

Separators commercially available	Effluent oil concentration (mg/1)
API rectangular	50-75
Circular	50-75
Inland Steel--Hydrogard	50-75
Shell PPI	35-50
Shell CPI	35-50
Finger-plate separator	35-50
Fram-Akers plate separator	50-100
Keene--Gravi-Pak	20

[*] Harris (1973, p. 85).

Rotational Separation--Successful separation of oil from water by utilizing rotational motion has been reported in the literature (Guzdar et al., 1975; Yu, 1969; Sinkin and Olney, 1956; Sheng and Welker, 1969). However, this separation method is practical and economical only when the concentrations of oil and suspended solids are high. Rotational separation is an accelerated gravity differential separation method and Stokes's Law applies; gravitational force is replaced by centrifugal force. The centrifugal force can be 1000 to 5000 times the gravity force, and the rate of separation is faster than in ordinary gravity separation. There are three basic types of rotational separators: (1) centrifuges, (2) hydrocyclones, and (3) vortex flow.

Centrifuges. Centrifuges have been used extensively in sludge-dewatering applications and for removal of solid contaminants from waste-waters. In recent applications, centrifuges have been used to separate oil from oil/water mixtures. In centrifugation, the oil/water mixture is moved along a circular path by the rotational motion of the device. The centrifugal force developed by rapid rotation of the system enhances the separation of the two phases. The phase with the higher density has a larger momentum and moves toward the outer periphery of the centrifuge; the less dense phase concentrates at the center line of the centrifuge. These phenomena occur as a result of the centrifugal force field and the difference in densities of the two phases. The greater the difference in the densities of the two phases, the faster the separation and the less the energy requirement. A minimum density difference of 5% is enough for separation. The location of the boundary between the two liquid phases can be predicted in theory, and it is possible to determine the critical oil-droplet size that will be present in the separated water phase.

Hydrocyclones. The basic principle of separation by a hydrocyclone is similar to that of a centrifuge. In a hydrocyclone, the liquid is forced into circular motion due to tangential injection of the oil/water mixture against the circular configuration of the hydrocyclone (Yu and Ventriglio, 1969). The advantages of a hydrocyclone over a centrifuge are low initial cost, ease of maintenance, and absence of moving parts. But hydrocyclones require considerable pumping power to achieve the centrifugal force needed for separation. Separation by a hydrocyclone is similar to vortex flow sep-aration, and problems associated with the turbulence created during operation have made both methods inefficient for treating oil/water mixtures.

Design--The design of centrifuges has not changed much since their first introduction. Emphasis is in providing centrifuges capable of achieving greater throughput, at low speed. The three types of centrifuges most often used in marine oil/water clarification applications are the barrel, tubular, and disc or plate types (Harris, 1973). Centrifuges can be designed for radial or axial flow. The Navy, Coast Guard, and Maritime Administration are sponsoring jointly a contract to develop a centrifuge. It is to incorporate axial flow, allowing for, comparatively high throughput and low speed. Axial flow design allows sufficient residence time for interdrop coalescence to occur, increasing the effectiveness of separation (Finger and Tabakin, 1973).

Performance--Oil/water separation by centrifugation is practical only when the oil and/or solid particles are present in relatively high concentra-tion and the densities of the oily and liquid phases are not close. Centri-fugation is effective in removing oil- and non-oil-coated suspended solids, free oil, and primary dispersions, if the average oil globule size is greater than the critical drop size. It is ineffective in removing stable emulsions and solubilized and dissolved oil. With chemical addition, this method has been used to destabilize and coalesce stable emulsions. Hence this method is

27

used mainly to concentrate and recover fuel oil from oily wastewaters with little water content. Finger and Tabakin (1973) report, in laboratory tests, effluent concentrations in the range of 10 ppm were obtained with feeds containing 1000 ppm of #2, #4, and Nigerian crude oil. At higher concentrations, ranging up to about 59,000 ppm of #2 oil and 19,000 ppm of #4 oil, effluent concentrations were higher, but did not exceed 100 ppm. The oil content of effluents reported by these authors is unusually low, and higher values should be expected. Efficiences of centrifuges are usually in the range 60-80%, depending on the specific nature of the oily wastes concerned, oil and suspended-solids concentrations, temperature, etc. The presence of detergents has an adverse effect on device performance.

Efficiencies ranging from 77 to 91% have been reported for hydrocyclones, but the oil content of effluents was persistently high and the separated oil phase contained water droplets (Sinkin and Olney, 1956). Sheng and Welker (1969) suggest the use of several hydrocyclone units, in a cascade operation, to produce effluents containing less than 100 ppm of oil; information on this process is currently not available. Centrifuges and hydrocyclones can be useful for gross separation, in lieu of more advanced and better separation methods.

Vortex flow. Separation of liquid/liquid mixtures, utilizing the fluid phenomenon known as confined vortex flow, can be achieved if the liquids differ in density. Vortex flow is similar to centrifugation; as such, it is an accelerated gravity settling technique. The separation of oil/water mixtures is accomplished by imparting relatively large rotational motion to the mixture, in a cylindrical vessel. As a result of the confined vortex flow, the lighter fluid (in most instances the oil) is accelerated radially inward faster than water. Therefore, oil accumulates and forms a central core, where it is removed by extraction tubes (or a perforated core) located at the center line of the cylinder.

Two types of vortex-flow separators are available commercially. In one type, the influent or recycle stream is injected tangentially into the cylinder through various inlet ports. Injection points are located at the circumference on one end of the cylinder. In the second type, a shrouded axial-flow pump impeller is used to rotate the fluid; this type is very similar to a centrifuge. However, vortex separation is different from centrifugation because the volume of fluid rotated at any time is smaller, and reinjection of some effluent water is necessary to maintain the vortex formed within the tube.

Design--Vortex separators consist primarily of a vortex tube, a cylindrical vessel with a perforated tube or extractor located at the center line, and have no moving parts. Important design parameters are: operating pressure, location of injection and exit ports, and length-to-width ratio of vortex tube. Several geometric variations are possible.

Performance--Several factors affect the performance of vortex-flow separators. These include: separator geometry, feed-oil concentration, oil type, oil-droplet-size distribution, debris, external motion, oil-collection rate, and temperature. In tests conducted with the United Aircraft vortex

28

separator, separation was poor; slightly emulsified oil could not be separated. Average oil content of effluents was above 50 ppm, and separated oil contained as much as 90% free water. Better separation was obtained when the unit was followed by a gravity separator. Because of physical limitations, vortex separation is capable of separating only free oil or oils with large droplet sizes. Even then, oil-removal efficiency can be lower than that of ordinary API gravity separators. Furthermore, injection of oil/water mixtures creates turbulence, which reduces oil-droplet sizes and hinders separation.

Gas Flotation--The success of gas flotation in the mineral industry led to its use for separating oil from wastewater (Gaudin, 1957). Gas flotation is an accelerated gravitational separation technique in which flotation of oil dispersions, wax and grease, and suspended solids in wastewater is accomplished by numerous microscopic gas bubbles. The process is a composite of the following steps (Vrablik, 1957):

a) introduction of gas bubbles into wastewater;
b) collisions between gas bubbles and suspended matter;
c) attachment of fine bubbles to the surfaces of suspended matter;
d) collisions between gas-attached suspended particles forming agglomerates;
e) entrapment of more gas bubbles into agglomerates; and
f) upward rise of floc structures in a "sweeping" action ("sweep flocculation").

A froth layer is formed at the surface of the wastewater and is removed by an appropriate skimming device.

The rise rate of the floc structures is expressed by a modified Stokes's Law:

$$v_o = \frac{gD_o^2(\delta_\omega - \delta_o)}{18\mu}$$

where v_o = rise rate of oil-air-particle agglomerates

g = gravitational constant

D_o = effective diameter of oil-air-particle agglomerates

δ_ω = density of aqueous phase

δ_o = density of oil-air-particle agglomerates

μ = absolute viscosity of aqueous phase.

The attachment of gas bubbles to suspended matter in the flotation process affects density and diameter in the Stokes's Law equation. The result is a net increase in rise rate. Two- to tenfold increases in rise rate are encountered, depending on other factors, e.g.,

a) gas-input rate and volume of gas released per unit volume of liquid;
b) bubble-size distribution and degree of dispersion;
c) surface properties of suspended matter;

29

d) hydraulic design of flotation chamber;
e) concentration and type of dissolved material;
f) concentration and type of suspended matter; and
g) temperature, pH, etc.

Different gases have been used for the flotation process (Vrablik, 1957; Berry and Engel, 1969), but flotation by air is most common. The essential property of the gas is limited solubility in water. Different flotation methods are practiced: dispersed air flotation, dissolved air flotation (DAF), vacuum desorption flotation, and electrochemical flotation. The first two methods differ in the way air is introduced to the wastewater; in the other two, the air bubbles are generated from the wastewater itself.

Dispersed air. In dispersed (diffused) air flotation, air is introduced through a special type of disperser (e.g., diffuser, sparger, revolving impellers, perforated tubes, etc.) to the influent of a flotation tank. The use of diffusers poses problems, particularly in oily wastewaters having high concentrations of suspended solids, waxes, and greases, because diffusers are susceptible to plugging. Air bubbles generated in dispersed air flotation have diameters of approximately 1000 µ and higher.

Dissolved air (DAF). In DAF, wastewater is saturated with air at an elevated pressure (usually 15 to 60 psig) in a retention tank for 1 to 5 minutes. Then, the pressure on the air-saturated wastewater is reduced to atmospheric, at the inlet to a flotation chamber. Reduction in pressure leads to the release of tiny air bubbles from solution. These have diameters ranging upwards from 50 µ. Retention time in the flotation chamber is about 15 minutes. Dissolving air in wastewater provides the maximum possible contact that can be established, and oil droplets or suspended particles may act as nucleation sites for bubble precipitation (Churchill, 1973). Three methods are used in operating DAF units: full-stream (total) pressurization, split-stream (partial) pressurization, and recycle-stream (recycle) pressurization. These three methods are shown in Figures 4 to 6. Each mode has its advantages and disadvantages (Churchill, 1973), but recycle-stream pressurization is considered superior to others (Rohlich, 1954; Simonsen, 1962). Typical recycle rates are about one-third of influent flow. Recycle units are the most common of all four flotation methods.

Vacuum desorption. Vacuum desorption flotation is accomplished in three steps (Rohlich, 1954):

a) a preaeration period to saturate wastewater with air at atmospheric pressure;
b) release of larger air bubbles; and
c) application of vacuum to the wastewater.

Depending on the vacuum applied, air bubbles have sizes similar to those in dissolved air flotation but, because of limited solubility, the desorption process may require higher energy than the dissolved flotation process. However, there is a reduction in turbulence relative to that which occurs in DAF units (flotation chamber). This turbulence is a deterrent to effective particle/bubble collisions.

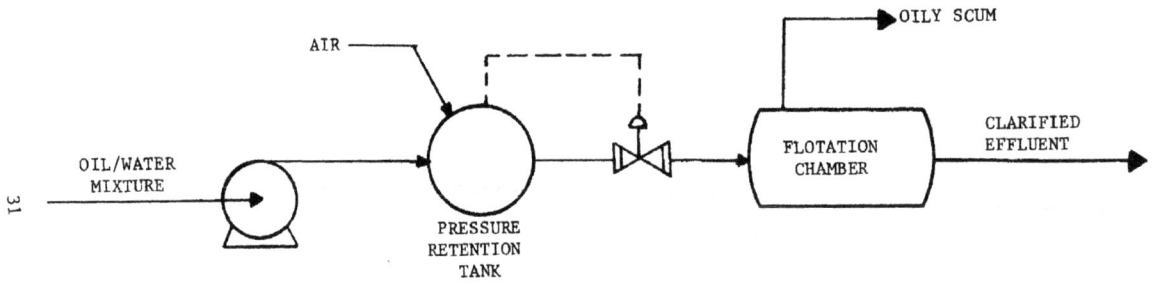

Figure 4. Total Pressurization System

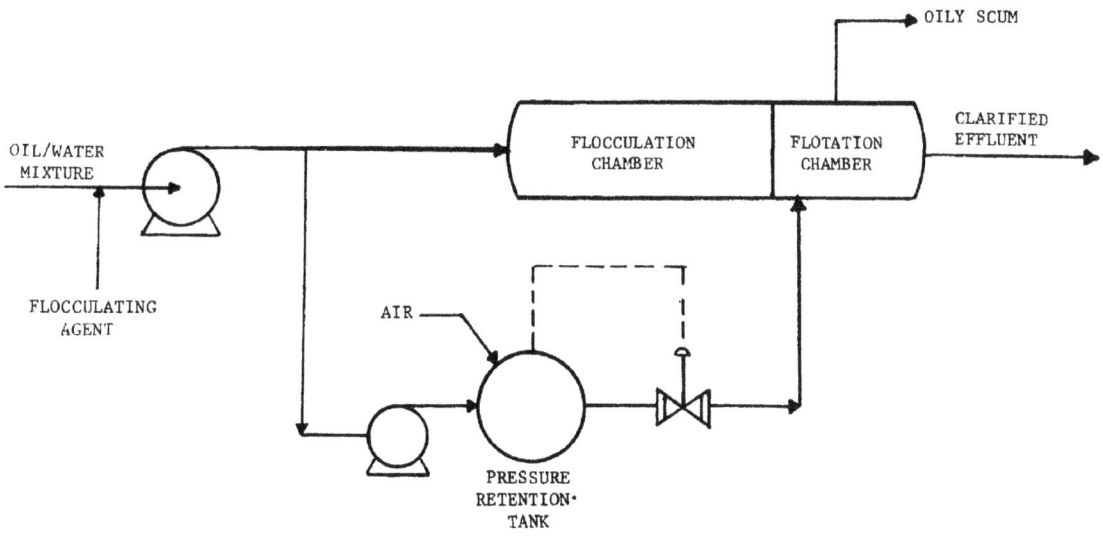

OIL/WATER
MIXTURE

FLOCCULATING
AGENT

AIR

PRESSURE
RETENTION·
TANK

FLOCCULATION
CHAMBER

FLOTATION
CHAMBER

OILY SCUM

CLARIFIED
EFFLUENT

32

Figure 5. Partial Pressurization System

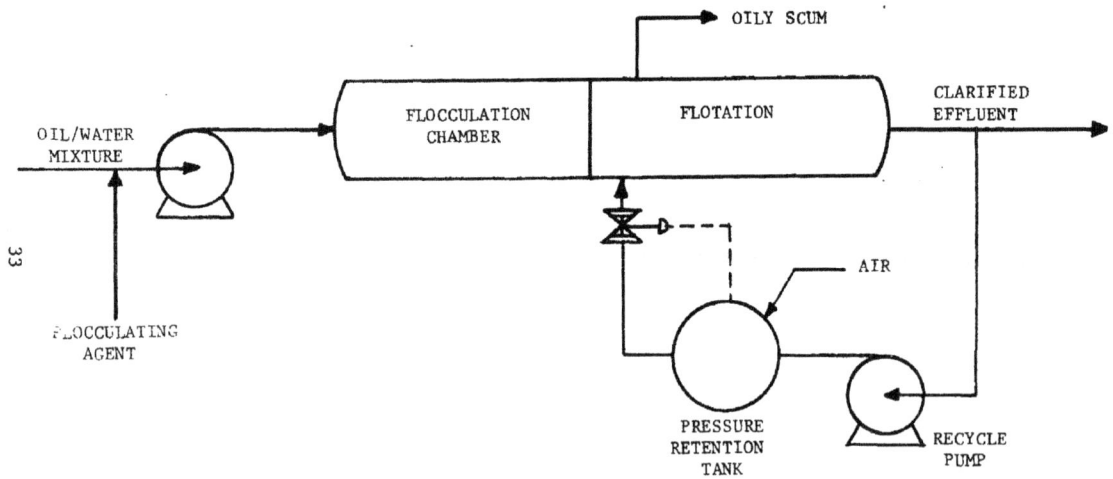

OILY SCUM

OIL/WATER
MIXTURE

FLOCCULATION
CHAMBER

FLOTATION

CLARIFIED
EFFLUENT

AIR

33

FLOCCULATING
AGENT

PRESSURE
RETENTION
TANK

RECYCLE
PUMP

Figure 6.   Recycle Pressurization System

Electrochemical. Electrochemical flotation is a recent concept. In this process, microgas bubbles are produced in wastewater by electrolysis. Bubble-size distribution is in the colloidal range, 0.001 to 0.1 μ; it is estimated that about 10 times as many bubbles are generated by this flotation process than are produced by air pressurization systems. Furthermore, gas bubbles produced electrolytically possess surface charges of either polarity. These surface charges can be effective in neutralizing oil dispersions and suspended solids stabilized by surface charges.

Design—Commercially available DAF units are rectangular or circular in shape and are constructed of steel. Important design parameters are: pressure, recycle ratio, inlet oil concentration, and residence time. DAF units generally consist of horizontal flow chambers, with inside configurations required for operation as gravity separators. The hydraulic design of DAF units is critical. Length-to-width ratios vary from 2/1 to 5/1. API has made recommendations on the design of DAF units (API Manual, 1969). Multicell DAF units are manufactured and are claimed to be more efficient than single-cell units (Ellis and Fisher, 1970). DAF units are generally more compact than API gravity separators.

Performance—Air flotation is used for removal of large oil globules and suspended solids. Flotation units are normally preceded by API gravity separators. The efficiency of air flotation depends. to a large extent, on air-bubble size. The gas bubbles are in a state of motion; collisions with suspended matter must occur before attachment takes place. If a suspended particle is much smaller than a bubble, the former may follow the viscous streamlines of the bubble and not make contact.

Because the bubble sizes expected in dispersed air flotation are of the order of 1000 μ, only unstable primary dispersions and large, oil-coated suspended solids will be separated. Consequently, oil-removal efficiencies lower than 25% and suspended-solids removal of about 20% can be achieved. Despite the smaller bubble-size distribution in DAF, oil-removal efficiencies are in the range of 60 to 90% (Stormont, 1956; Quigley and Hoffman, 1966). Suspended-solids removal as high as 95% have been reported. Particles exhibiting neutral buoyancy may be removed by flotation, if they are not stabilized by surface charges. D'Arcy (1951) reported an unusually high final effluent quality (between 5 and 7 ppm). If properly designed and operated, oil concentrations of effluents from DAF units can be kept below 50 ppm.

The efficiencies of vacuum desorption flotation units are generally lower than those of DAF units, even when high vacuums are used. Electrochemical flotation may be capable of separating oil droplets and suspended solids stabilized by surface charges.

Motion during the separation process has significant effect on device performance; motion interferes with skimming of the froth layer. Floated oil and solids may redisperse in the aqueous phase. For an efficient separation, oil concentration in influent should not vary significantly.

Filtration

Filtration through granular materials is one of the oldest methods for separating oil/water mixtures. This technique is useful for removing suspended matter and associated materials, particularly oil, from oily wastewaters. It is best suited for removing oil-coated solids that are a major cause of fouling in coalescing devices. Neutrally buoyant oil-coated solids that may require infinite settling times can be removed, also. As a result, this technique is becoming very important in the petroleum industry because of its capacity to reduce the concentration of oil and level of suspended solids in production waters that are passed, subsequently, to secondary and tertiary recovery operations.

The mechanisms involved in removal of suspended solids by filtration are very complex and little understood. With deep granular filters of coarse material, removal is primarily within the filter bed (commonly referred to as depth filtration). Some solids may be removed by a process of interstitial straining, and oil may be removed by adsorption on the bed material.

There are three main filtration techniques: layer, membrane, and fibrous-media. Membrane filtration is discussed in the section on membrane processes, and filtration by fibrous media is essentially a coalescence/filtration technique which has been discussed elsewhere. The present discussion focuses on layer filtration only. Layer filtration can be divided into two types: deep granular and multimedia.

Layer Filtration--Granular media. Several materials have been used as granular media; these include sand, crushed anthracite coal, perlite, diatomaceous earth, garnet or ilmenite sand, and powdered or granular activated carbon. A granular-media filter normally utilizes a bed of these materials to remove the contaminant. The most common and economical filter material is fine, graded sand (slow and rapid sand filtration). The effective size of the filter media may vary from 0.35 to 1.0 mm. In the backwash cycle, hydraulic grading of the sand occurs, with the finest sand forming the top of the bed. Therefore, if a suspended solid present in the process stream is not trapped in the top layer, it is most likely to be found in the effluent because larger voids occur in the direction of liquid flow.

Multimedia. To overcome the shortcomings of layered systems, multimedia filters were introduced. The principle of multimedia filtration is that coarser grains of lower specific gravity will settle more slowly than heavier but finer grains, during the backwash cycle, provided the size ratio between different materials is properly selected (Hsiung et al., 1974). With dual media, combinations of two materials are used, e.g. crushed anthracite coal and silica sand. The dual media have the largest grains (coal) at the top and the smaller sand grains below, but the average grain size at the bottom is still relatively large.

To decrease average grain size, mixed-media filters are used. A mixed-media filter uses three or more materials, each of different size and density, that intermix, not stratify, to form a filter grading from coarse at the top to fine at the bottom in the direction of flow. Typically, anthracite coal, silica sand, and garnet are used (Evers, 1975). The main advantage of using mixed-media filters is pressure-drop reduction at 'high' flow rates, without deterioration of effluent quality. Longer filter runs can be achieved, also. Increasing the number of filter materials (different densities and sizes) approaches an ideal filter, one in which the size of media particles decreases uniformly. However, the additional advantages of the ideal filter, for three-media or four-media cases, do not offset the extra cost.

Design--Deep granular filters consist generally of 18 to 30 inches of filter medium. The filter material is supported on an under-drain system inside a pressure or gravity-flow vessel. Concrete systems are available, also.

The design of mixed-media filters depends on several factors: the desired effluent quality, the oil and suspended-solids content of feed, desired flow rate, and maximum allowable head loss. An excellent filter can be made from 18 inches of 1.0-mm "effective"-size coal (sp. gr. 1.6), 0.5-mm "effective"-size sand (sp. gr. 2.6), and 0.3-mm "effective"-size garnet (sp. gr. 4.0). The size and quantity of each filter material can be varied independently to meet specific requirements. The average oil-droplet and suspended-solids sizes are the primary determinants of the size of the various materials used. After the first backwash, the materials become intermixed but the filtration efficiency increases in the direction of liquid flow. Typical filtration rates are 5 to 10 gal/min/sq ft. The preferred surface wash system is the rotating-arm type; during backwash, the bed is expanded at least 15% for efficient cleaning. Air wash is sometimes used for cleaning mixed media, but it is not as effective as backwashing unless sufficient water is provided for fluidization of the filter, after the air scour. Multistage filters are being designed, so there is no interruption of operation during backwash of one unit. Devices are equipped with automatic backwash systems which initiate backwash cycles on a time cycle or on the basis of filter head loss.

Performance--Oil-removal efficiency and storage capacity of a filter depend upon the media design. Filters have a limited oil-retention capacity, and when effluent quality deteriorates and becomes unacceptable, or when pressure drop through the filter reaches a predetermined value, operation is discontinued and filters must be washed to restore capacity. Literature on the subject of backwashing filters used for oil removal shows that fouling of media is a common problem. Fouling results from the accumulation of suspended solids within the bed and/or from biological growth in the bed. Caking or mud-balling in filters is common; filters are not well suited for intermittent flows. Failure of automatic backwashing devices is a major cause of poor effluent quality. Scheduling, or backwash frequency, constitutes a problem, also. Properly designed surface-wash and backwash facilities can keep filter media clean over prolonged periods of use.

Tests using multimedia filtration to precondition production waters for reinjection during secondary and tertiary recovery operations indicate the absence of visible oil in effluents. Pilot tests conducted at the University of Houston indicate that mixed-media filters are very effective in separating

36

unstable oil/water emulsions formed by pumping light Iranian crude oil into the suction side of a fresh-water feed pump. This filter was operated at 10 to 12 gal/min/sq ft, with an influent containing 750 ppm of oil; COD measurements indicated a 95 to 100% oil-removal efficiency, in runs of up to 6 hours. With 100 ppm of oil in the feed, a run lasted more than 30 hours and effluent contained about 10 to 20 ppm of oil (COD measurements). Tests of a deep-bed sand filter at the same loading rate indicated an oil-removal efficiency of 85 to 90%, when the feed contained 250 ppm of oil. A filter run lasted about 16 hours (Hooper and Myrick, 1972). It should be noted, however, that the very long operating times and high oil-retaining capability of the bed were probably due to the absence of suspended solids in the feed.

Results of these tests show that filtration using granular materials is a candidate for separating oil/water mixtures containing unstable emulsions, oil-coated solids in suspension, and some free oil. However, the process generates secondary wastes (backwash) which have to be treated before discharge. The volumes of such wastes are generally small. When used in conjunction with chemical treatment, filtration can separate chemically stabilized oil emulsions but, because of physical limitations, dissolved oil will still be present in effluents from devices operating on the filtration principle.

Membrane--During the last decade, there has been rapid progress in the development of artificial membranes. As a result, membrane processes are becoming increasingly important in wastewater treatment. Hydrophobic and hydrophilic membranes have been used for oil/water separation, particularly for polishing purposes, because membrane fouling is a major problem. For efficient separation, the membrane has to be matched to the oil/water system to be separated, and the feed must be free from suspended solids. Pore size and structure of the membrane determine the quality of effluent. Membrane processes for separating oil/water mixtures are still in the developmental state; some of their disadvantages are limited rates and throughputs achievable and high cost. Processes are slow, but effluents from membrane devices usually have oil content below acceptable discharge limit.

Membrane processes are different from conventional microporous filtration. Membranes are semipermeable, extremely fine in porosity, and easily fouled. Depending on a membrane's surface characteristics, it will pass oil but not water, or vice versa. If the viscosity of the oily phase is too high for passage through a membrane at a practical rate at ambient temperature, a method has to be devised for heating the feed mixture. The energy requirement for processing large volumes of wastewater is large. If the oily phase has a low viscosity, a large surface area is required to process a volume of wastewater. Therefore, membrane processes are prohibitively expensive and can be justified only for handling small-volume wastewaters or for removing the last traces of oil, notably soluble oils and chemically stabilized emulsions. In membrane processes, little pretreatment of feed is necessary. New membranes are being developed that can process untreated feeds. As the research activity currently in progress yields good results, and if membranes can be made cheaply, membrane processes will become more attractive and may eventually replace other treatment and separation methods because of the high-quality effluents that are possible.

37

The major membrane processes are electrodialysis, reverse osmosis, and ultrafiltration.

Electrodialysis. Electrodialysis has been used extensively for desalting applications. The driving force for this technique is electrical potential gradient; separation is based on selective ion transport across a membrane. The flow of electrical current in electrodialysis causes water to flow (electro-osmosis) and to be separated from the oil phase by a water-selective membrane across the current path. Desired membrane properties are high water-transport number, high electrical conductivity, good chemical resistivity, and high mechanical strength. Electrodialysis has not been investigated extensively as a possible separation technique, but it may be useful for separating wastewaters containing emulsions stabilized by surface charges. This technique may be practical for small-volume wastewaters; however, pretreatment of feed will be necessary to diminish membrane plugging. Some of the disadvantages of this technique are high energy requirements, dissociation of water at high current densities, imperfectly selective membranes, low liquid flow rates, and concentration polarization. These phenomena reduce the overall efficiency of this technique.

Reverse osmosis. Like electrodialysis, reverse osmosis has found application to desalting operations for brackish water. The principal driving force for this technique is pressure; reverse osmosis is essentially a membrane filtration technique, in which pressures are greater than the osmotic pressure exerted by species in solution. Separation is on the basis of molecular size. Applied pressure forces water, and species smaller in size than the rejection level of the membrane, through the membrane. Oil and larger species will be rejected at the membrane surface. The smaller the size of the species present in the oily wastewater, the greater the osmotic pressure generated; therefore, reverse osmosis has an added advantage of being able to remove species of atomic dimensions by using tight membranes and operating pressures higher than the osmotic pressure. Experiments have shown that conventional dialysis membranes of the semipermeable, molecular diffusion type are not appropriate for use in reverse osmosis. Cellulose acetate membranes are presently used most widely. New casting techniques have led to production of ordinary and modified cellulose acetate membranes which appear adequate for reverse osmosis processes on the bases of high water flux and good rejection of organic molecules. A wide variety of membranes and backing systems is being developed. One important commercial system is based on a polyamide membrane. Fluxes greater than 25 gal/day/sq ft of membrane are possible, at applied pressures up to 1500 psig. One problem encountered is the slow decrease, with time, of oil rejection because of membrane hydrolysis. As a result, operation is applicable to a narrow pH range, to increase membrane life. Fouling is not a serious problem because rejected matter is usually passed downstream by the flowing process stream, but periodic cleaning is necessary.

Ultrafiltration. Ultrafiltration is similar to reverse osmosis, differing because it is not impeded by osmotic pressure. Reverse osmosis systems operate at elevated pressures of 250 to 1500 psig, while ultrafiltration systems are operated at lower pressures of only 50 to 200 psig. Because of lower operating pressures, ultrafiltration membranes are more open, and rejection of only colloidal or suspended matter and other macromolecules is possible. The predominant mechanism in ultrafiltration is selective sieving through pores. In the ultrafiltration process, feed is pumped through the center of a porous tube on which a membrane has been cast integrally. Hydraulic pumping pressure causes water and some dissolved, low molecular weight materials to pass; however, emulsified oil, free oil, and oil-coated solids are retained and concentrated in the tube. To be useful for ultrafiltration, membranes must have a narrow molecular weight cutoff and a high solvent flux at low-pressure differentials. Early work in ultrafiltration was done using cellophane or porous cellulose nitrate membranes, but reproducibility was poor; adsorption on pore walls and plugging were common. Because of breakthroughs in membrane technology, a variety of synthetic polymeric membranes is being tested in the ultrafiltration process. The most promising, thus far, are non-cellulosic in nature and allow operation over a wide range of pH and temperature. The limitations of this process are flux decline with time and the phenomenon of concentration polarization. Flux decline is the sum of membrane compaction and fouling. Economic studies have shown that the most fruitful areas for significant gains are higher water fluxes and longer membrane life.

Design--Ultrafiltration and reverse osmosis plants consist of a series-parallel arrangement of modules. About four different module designs are possible: plate and frame, tubular, spiral-wound, and hollow-fiber configuration. Fibers are housed in cartridges that allow for expansion. A detailed comparison of module designs has been investigated and summarized by Schatzberg et al. (1975). Ease of cleaning modules varies and backflushing systems, with or without detergent cleaning, are incorporated into some of the newer units. A typical membrane has an asymmetric structure, consisting of a thin, dense skin on a porous support. It is approximately 100 µ thick, with a surface skin of approximately 0.2 µ that acts as the rejecting surface. The pore size is of the order of 5 to 50 Å and, thus, is approximately 1000 times smaller than emulsified oil droplets (Nordstrom, 1974).

Generally, the membrane must be maintained wet at all times, although some of the newer membranes can be handled dry. More recently, there has been a trend toward development of thin-channel hollow fibers (Messinger, 1974). Hollow-fiber reverse osmosis systems are smaller in size than ultrafiltration systems, but require greater power inputs (Finger and Tabakin, 1973). Ultrafiltration systems can be operated in batch or continuous modes; throughput rates are usually small in both cases. Permeate rates in ultrafiltration are higher than obtainable in reverse osmosis systems.

Performance--Applications of reverse osmosis and ultrafiltration systems to the separation of oily wastewaters have been investigated (Desai, 1971; Goldsmith and Hossain, 1973; Nordstrom, 1974; Schatzberg et al., 1975). Results of these tests indicate good separation, even though membrane processes are still in the developmental stage. Studies at the Naval Ship Research and Development Center, Annapolis, with reverse osmosis systems, reveal that treated oily wastewater, containing 500 ppm of oil, gave an effluent containing approximately 10 ppm of oil. Permeate fluxes ranged from 10 to 25 gal/day/sq ft, but periodic cleaning was necessary to minimize decline in permeate rates as a result of fouling (Finger and Tabakin, 1973). Results of experiments with ultrafiltration systems tested at the Center showed 90% oil-removal efficiency, with a feed containing 100 ppm of oil. Permeate was free of emulsified oil and contained less than 10 ppm of dissolved oil. Membrane fouling was a problem, and only a detergent wash restored membrane flux capacity. Finger and Tabakin (1973) note that chemically emulsified oil wastes from bilge cleaning would actually improve ultrafiltration, by minimizing fouling, but detergents are known to cause membrane disintegration. Membrane processes are very useful for separating stable emulsions, oil-coated solids, and free oil. Processes can achieve close to 100% oil-removal efficiency, if adequately maintained and operated. Removal of dissolved oils cannot be achieved in these systems but, with the advent of tighter membranes capable of withstanding very large operating pressures, reverse osmosis will become a candidate for separating dissolved oil. Ultrafiltration and reverse osmosis are expensive processes, throughputs are low, and membrane replacement is necessary as a result of fouling and other aging factors. It is possible to minimize concentration polarization in ultrafiltration by operating at high feed velocities parallel to the membrane surface and/or utilizing thin-channel hollow fibers.

Coalescence/Filtration

Coalescence of dispersed oils in aqueous suspension occurs in almost all liquid/liquid separation processes. Originally, the coalescence process was used to remove water from oil in aerosol filtration and, because it was successful, it was adapted for removing oil from oil/water mixtures. The term, as used in this report, refers to the coalescence process induced by flow through porous media. Coalescence is a complicated operation; it has been studied extensively, but the phenomenon is not completely understood (Jordan, 1953; Voyutskii et al., 1955, 1958; Redmon, 1963; Farley and Valentin, 1965; Sareen et al., 1966; Spielman, 1968; Spielman and Goren, 1972a,b). Several theories have been advanced to explain the mechanism of coalescence (Vinson, 1965; Hazlett, 1969a, Jeffreys and Davies, 1971).

The following major steps were proposed by Voyutskii et al. (1955):

a) collisions of emulsion globules with the ends of filter fibers;
b) adhesion of droplets to the fiber;
c) coalescence of the microdrops;
d) adhesion of microdrops to the surfaces of fibers; and
e) trickling of coalesced drops down the fibers.

Hazlett (1969a) proposed dividing the coalescence process into three main steps: approach of a droplet to a fiber or to a droplet attached to a fiber, attachment of a droplet to a fiber or to a droplet already attached to a fiber, and release of an enlarged droplet from the fiber surface. Each step involves considerable complexity or alternative mechanisms. The fibers and coalesced liquid matrix may capture droplets by a number of mechanisms: interception, Brownian diffusion, inertial impaction, gravity settling, and long-range attractive forces. Except for small particles, interception is considered the dominant mechanism (Spielman and Goren, 1970). Therefore, in

40

coalescence, oil dispersions are retained in the porous media where the drops grow larger, until they are large enough to be swept away by fluid-flow forces. Coalesced oil snakes through the porous media until it reaches the downstream face of the media, where it is released in individual droplets large enough to separate from the aqueous medium by gravity.

Jordan (1965) classified liquid/liquid coalescing into two general types:

a) depth-type: the coalescing operation occurs within the porous material and both phases of the liquid system pass through the porous material; and

b) surface-type: coalescence occurs on the surface of the porous material and only one liquid phase passes through the porous material.

Surface-type coalescence and ordinary filtration are similar. In fact, some filtration occurs in any coalescence process. Therefore, devices operating on the coalescence principle are often called filter-coalescers.

A wide variety of materials has been used as coalescing media: natural fibers (cotton and wool), synthetic materials (fiber glass, viscose, nylon, orlon, and felt), reticulated (open-pore) foams, membranes (hydrolyzed and cellulose acetate), screens, mats, and granular materials (pebbles, sand, and diatomaceous earth). Because of the complex nature of coalescence, various approaches to coalescence processes have been identified. The major differences in these modes are almost entirely the type of porous media used.

Fibrous-Media--Coalescence using fibrous media is the most important of the coalescence types mentioned above. Fibrous materials with different internal, geometric, and surface properties have been used. Voyutskii et al. (1958) used viscose and wool fibers. Cotton and glass wool were used by Gudesen (1964). The most common fibrous material in use is fiber glass (Burtis and Kirkbride, 1946; Hayes et al., 1949; Graham, 1962; Rose, 1963; Sweeney, 1964). Coalescence performance of fiber glass can be enhanced by coating the fiber surfaces with certain synthetic resins, e.g. phenolic resins, to render them hydrophobic or hydrophilic. The use of fibrous media implies depth-type coalescence.

Membrane--Membrane coalescence belongs to the surface-type discussed above. Several separatory membranes are available. Membrane materials are usually such that they can be treated to render them hydrophobic or hydrophilic. Liquid flow rates are small. Membrane coalescence devices are normally preceded by fibrous-bed coalescers, i.e. they are used as polishing stages. This mode is similar to membrane filtration and is covered in that discussion.

Centrifuge--As mentioned, gravity separation is an integral part of the coalescence process. In centrifugal coalescence, fibrous material is used as the coalescing medium, but the final gravity separation of the oil and water phases is enhanced by centrifugation. Literature on this technique has been reviewed.

Bimetallic--Coalescence of dilute o/w emulsions by passage of the mixture through a bed containing a granular mixture of dissimilar metals (iron and aluminum) or carbon and a metal is a new concept proposed by Fowkes et al. (1970). Various bimetal and carbon-metal beds have been tested, but no complete engineering assessment of this technique's potential has been reported. The process is essentially an electrokinetic phenomenon (Koelmans and Overbeek, 1954), similar to electrophoresis and electrodeposition, but it has coalescence/filtration characteristics (Ghosh and Brown, 1975).

Granular-Media--Beds of gravel, pebble or sand have been investigated as coalescing media for oil/water separation (Douglas and Elliot, 1962; Shackleton et al., 1960). Coalescence using diatomaceous earth and other granular materials has been reported. This type of coalescence process is discussed further in the section on layer filtration.

Other Porous Materials--Fine-mesh screens, non-woven mattings (polyester felt, polypropylene felt, and glass mats) and reticulated foams have been used as coalescence media (Vinson, 1965; The Permutit Company, 1966; Chieu et al., 1975). In this coalescence process and that using granular media, oil droplets are adsorbed until the bed is saturated or the breakthrough oil concentration in effluent is reached. Then, operation is discontinued so that adsorbed oil can be removed by backwashing or squeezing the media.

Design of Fibrous-Media Coalescers--Since the mechanisms which lead to coalescence are not fully understood, design of filter-coalescers is largely empirical. The most common configuration for fibrous-media coalescers is a cartridge. Fibers are arranged and bonded together to provide a tortuous path for fine oil droplets in order to achieve reliable coalescence (Finger and Tabakin, 1973; Freestone and Tabakin, 1975). Desired properties of cartridge elements are: uniform structure, sufficient pore openings, and adequate mechanical strength to withstand operating pressures of 25 to 75 psig. The direction of liquid flow through the coalescing element is usually radially outward. Cartridges (filter elements) are housed in cylindrical vessels that can be mounted vertically or horizontally.

Coalescing elements are available in different sizes depending on unit capacity. Coalescing devices normally contain more than one cartridge, each cartridge can be removed independently, and the entire unit can be assembled easily. Fiber sizes vary from less than 5-μ to 25-μ diameter. Failures of cartridge-type coalescers occur as a result of improper end-cap sealing (poor end cap-to-element sealing and/or poor gasket-to-end cap sealing) and poor quality control (defective elements and voids in filter media). Because of the problems associated with solids, most devices are equipped with a screen or prefilter ahead of the coalescer elements. The main purpose of the prefilter is to remove solid particles that may plug the pores of the coalescing filter elements. However, the prefilter also acts as a coalescing filter and preconditions the feed. Coarse filter cartridges, with approximately 25- to 100-μ-diameter fibers, are used as prefilters.

Since gravity separation is an integral part of coalescence, commercially available coalescers are multistaged. The first stage is used as a gross gravity separator or may contain a prefilter. Succeeding stages alternate

42

coalescence and gravity separation. Important design parameters are: amount of fibrous material (voidage), arrangement of fibers, and hydrodynamic factors.

Coalescers are compact and easily assembled, and operation is flexible. They are usually not regenerated through fluidization or backwashing; therefore, replacement of coalescing elements is necessary. Coalescers equipped with automatic cartridge-cleaning devices are available commercially. Figure 7 is a schematic diagram of a cartridge filter/coalescer.

Performance of Fibrous-Media Coalescers—In coalescence, a principal driving force is interfacial tension (Yu and Ventriglio, 1969). Lowering the interfacial tension of the oil and water phases promotes coalescence of the dispersed oil phase. But coalescence can also occur in systems having high interfacial tension, if the density difference between the two phases is high and coalescing surfaces have a high degree of roughness (Jeffreys and Davies, 1971). Attempts have been made to analyze the performance of fibrous-bed coalescers using filter coefficients. Theoretical expressions for filter coefficients have been developed by several investigators using various coalescence models (Spielman and Goren, 1970, 1972a,b; Sherony and Kientner, 1971; Rosenfeld and Wasan, 1974). Important coalescing parameters are:

a) physical properties of coalescing media-preferential wettability of bed, bed-spreading characteristics, fiber size, packing, pore-size distribution, uniformity of structure, surface roughness of fibers, and two-phase permeability of bed;
b) interfacial tension and contact angle;
c) flow velocity; and
d) physicochemical properties of fluids (viscosity, density, temperature, etc.).

Combinations of small- and large-size fibers improve oil-removal efficiency, if the larger-size fibers are located at the downstream end of the cartridge (Voyutskii, 1958; Hazlett, 1969b; Jeffreys and Davies, 1971). Resins used in bonding fibers together usually give an intermediate contact angle (Hazlett, 1969a). Preferentially oil-wetted mats are believed to be less efficient than aqueous-wetted mats for separation of o/w emulsions (Spielman and Goren, 1972b). Voyutskii (1955) found a critical flow velocity, less than 1 cm/sec, below which separation was possible. Gloyna and Ford (1974) found that oil-removal efficiency of coalescers is related to two major factors:

a) variation in type of oil, degree of emulsion, droplet size, and suspended-solids concentration; and
b) fluctuations in flow rates, influent oil concentration, and equipment upsets.

For successful operation of filter beds, it is important that solid particles are removed from the oil/water mixtures before passage through the bed. Solid matter deposited in the bed will not only change the voidage and local fluid velocities in the bed but, more important, the surface properties of the bed will be changed. Particulate matter (suspended solids and

43

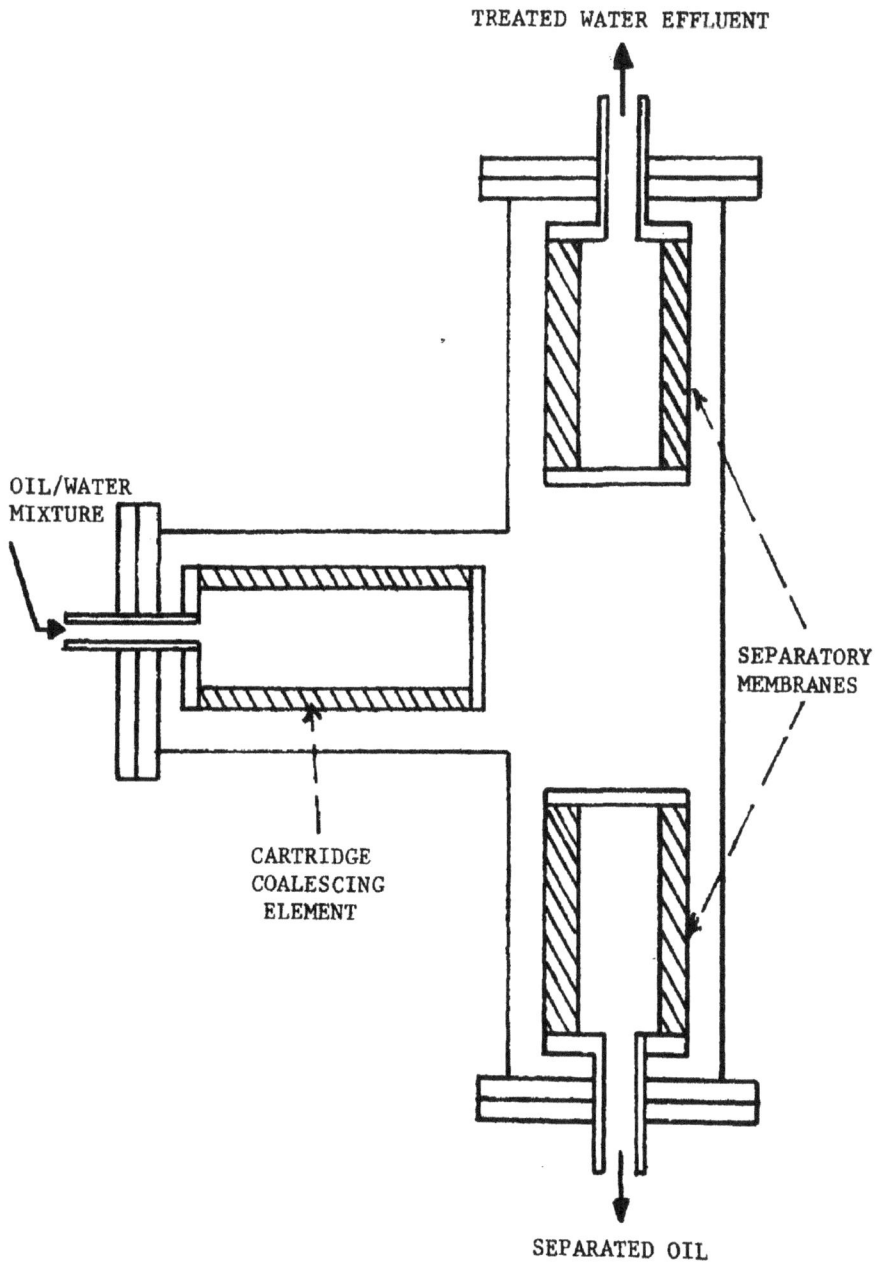

TREATED WATER EFFLUENT

OIL/WATER
MIXTURE

SEPARATORY
MEMBRANES

CARTRIDGE
COALESCING
ELEMENT

SEPARATED OIL

Figure 7. A Complete Liquid/Liquid Coalescing System

44

gelatinous materials) interferes with effective coalescing. Plugging of coalescing media often is the cause of coalescer failure. Plugging results in an increase in head loss and coalescer elements require elaborate cleaning to restore efficient separation or replacement of filter elements.

The effects of surfactants on coalescence have not been studied extensively. Detergents concentrate at the oil/water interface during coalescence (Lindenhofen and Shertzer, 1967), limit droplet growth prior to detachment, and hinder droplet release from the downstream face of the filter (Hazlett, 1969b). It has been suggested that surfactants degrade coalescer performance by absorption on the fibers, resulting in an increase in the contact angle and decrease in wettability (Hazlett, 1969b). This alteration of the surface properties of the coalescing fibers leads to poisoning of the coalescer and eventual failure.

Coalescers are particularly suited for removal of oil dispersions, but segregating phases after separation is difficult and expensive. Small quantities of water may be present in the separated oily effluent of coalescers. Oil content of influents to coalescers should be limited to 200 ppm and should fluctuate only within a narrow range. However, if coalescers are well operated and maintained, oil-removal efficiencies can be as high as 99%. Typical values are higher than 90%. Results of studies at the Annapolis evaluation facility indicate that 10 ppm of oil in effluent water can be attained with some commercially available coalescers (Finger and Tabakin, 1973). Coalescers are not designed to remove dissolved and non-colloidal oils (solubilized oil); therefore, oil/water mixtures containing these systems cannot be treated effectively. Oil dispersions stabilized by surface charges cannot be treated adequately, although bimetallic coalescers have a potential for treating this system. Solids, stabilized oil emulsions, and suspended slimy materials, if present in influents to coalescers, may reduce efficiencies below those obtained with gravity separators (Gloyna and Ford, 1974).

Adsorption and Absorption

Sorption on solids, particularly activated carbon, has become a widely used operation for purification of waters and wastewaters. Activated carbon has an affinity for organic matter present in petrochemical and refinery wastewaters and, thus, is an effective means of removing dissolved oil, solubilized oil, and chemically stabilized emulsions that cannot be destabilized by chemical addition and other methods. These oil/water systems pose serious problems in various oil/water separating devices.

Activated carbon has demonstrated large adsorptive capacity and desired surface properties, making it adequate for adsorption processes; it is the material most widely used. Adsorption is an interface phenomenon; oil is selectively adsorbed on the surface of the carbon, but the adsorbed film is only a few molecules thick. Adsorption of oil molecules from the aqueous phase to the carbon surface occurs as a result of a combination of various forces: adhesive, cohesive, electrical, surface tension, and van der Waals. Contact between carbon surfaces and oil wastewater is achieved through fixed-bed or expanded-bed carbon columns. As adsorption of oil and other organic matter present in the waste stream is accomplished, the carbon loses its adsorptive capacity and breakthrough occurs. Spent carbon must be replaced or reactivated. The process is uneconomical if the spent carbon is wasted; therefore, it must be reactivated and reused with new carbon added to make up the losses of regeneration. Regeneration is an extremely important consideration in the use of activated carbon for treatment of oily wastewaters. Currently, regenerative methods are mainly thermal. The regenerative process requires a large capital investment and has high operational costs. It is presently feasible to regenerate carbon, by conventional thermal techniques, for several cycles of successful saturation and regeneration. The feasibility of other regenerative techniques is being investigated. These are (1) the use of steam to drive off the adsorbed oil and (2) repeated washings of the spent carbon with solvents. The results of these attempts have been disappointing because of high cost and the small efficiency achieved.

Design--The basic design and operating concepts of gravity flow, pressure, and expanded-bed-type-flow adsorbers are essentially similar to those for granular-bed filters of the corresponding types. Fixed-bed units are usually vertical pressure vessels containing activated carbon supported on an under-drain system. Important design considerations are flow rate, contact time, depth of carbon, influent oil and suspended-solids concentrations, and desired effluent quality. Multiple adsorption columns are usually provided in series or in parallel so that a unit can be taken out for regeneration. Moving-bed carbon adsorption columns are also being used to eliminate the spare columns required for regeneration. Chiyoda, Japan, uses a new method of contacting carbon and wastewater. Unlike conventional fixed-bed systems, the Chiyoda multistage, fluidized-bed system is based on a unique process in which activated carbon is circulated in continuous, countercurrent contact with the wastewater and, when spent, carbon is reactivated for recirculation. The advantage of this system is the absence of the removal of spent carbon and replenishment with fresh carbon. The system can be operated without interruption. Design is compact, space requirements are reduced, and there is a flexibility of future expansion (Chiyoda Company, 1974).

Performance--If properly operated, carbon adsorption columns provide effluents that will meet practically all discharge limits for oil. Pilot tests conducted by the Ben Holt Company, California, using carbon adsorption columns in lieu of coalescing devices, indicated oil and surfactant present in the influent were removed efficiently. Feed to the combined system was typical Navy oily waste containing seawater, oil, sludge, dirt, and chemically stabilized emulsion. Influent to the carbon columns had an oil content varying from 35 to 530 ppm. The highest effluent oil content was 2.5 ppm, measured by chloroform extraction and IR spectrophotometry. Surfactant concentration at the carbon inlet varied from 63 to 630 ppm and was removed to a level not detectable by IR analysis (Ben Holt Company, 1974). Feasibility studies of variations of the adsorption process by Calspan Corporation, New York, showed efficient separations. In the latter studies, carbon adsorption was used in conjunction with plain sedimentation, dissolved air flotation, mixing and filtration, and polyelectrolyte coagulation. The average oil content of effluents was 1 ppm, with contact times of less than 3 minutes and influents containing up to 2000 ppm of oil. All samples were analyzed for oil content by percent transmittance measurement. Though results showed efficient separation, the carbon dosages required were quite large: 1 g of activated carbon per liter of wastewater (Wang et al., 1973).

Oil-removal efficiencies in carbon adsorption are usually very high: in the range 95 to 100%; a typical value is 98%. An obvious disadvantage of the simple adsorption process is low capacity, necessitating huge surface areas. Therefore, carbon adsorption columns are used as polishing stages in lieu of other separators. Removal of suspended solids is accomplished, also, because of the filtration characteristics of carbon columns. However, in spite of the high efficiencies achievable with this process, it has not found wide-spread use because of the large expenditure involved. Attempts to use coke, instead of activated carbon, as the absorption medium and to regenerate a saturated adsorption surface by coking have not provided any encouragement (Freestone and Tabakin, 1975). Nonetheless, carbon adsorption has proven to be the answer where other physical and chemical treatment techniques have failed and, as wastewater control regulations become more stringent, the process has become indispensable.

Electric and Magnetic Separation

Separation of oil from water by electric and magnetic means has not been fully investigated because of the high cost involved and the low liquid flow rates achievable in such devices. These disadvantages, together with the technological problems encountered, have made these methods unattractive. The two methods in this category are electrophoresis and magnetization.

Electrophoretic--Electrophoretic separation has been used in oil refineries for recovering oil from oil-rich wastewaters, but its application has been limited to processing small volumes of wastes in which w/o emulsions are the major contaminant. Electrophoresis, an electrokinetic phenomenon, is the principle of separation in this technique. A strong electrical field is established in the wastewater; dispersed particles move along the lines of force and become separated from the continuous medium because of the net electrical charge on each particle. The electrophoretic mobility of a water particle is greater than that of an oil globule of the same size. Therefore, this method is practical for separating w/o emulsions which are produced during drilling operations. This method becomes more effective as the sizes of the water droplets become smaller. When the water droplets are larger than 10 μ in size, a considerable electrical energy has to be used for an appreciable separation to occur. An increase in the energy requirement can lead to hydrolysis of water; hydrogen and/or chlorine gas may be generated at the electrodes. Gas generation makes the wastewater turbulent and further degrades separation efficiency. Separation of oil-in-seawater emulsions is difficult because of the high electrical conductivity of seawater and the possibility of concentration polarization. In general, electrophoretic separation is a slow, inefficient process and is not suitable for the treatment of large volumes of oily wastewater.

Magnetic--The feasibility of recovering oil from fine, stable, o/w emulsions by magnetic means has been investigated by Kaiser et al. (1971). In operation, a ferrofluid is added to the wastewater to make the dispersed oily phase magnetically responsive. The wastewater is passed through a packed bed placed in a magnetic field. Packed beds are composed of magnetic particles or screens. Results of experiments indicate virtually complete removal of oil particles, as small as 1 μ in diameter, using air-gap fields of several thousand oersteds, bed packing of several inches in length, and oil-phase magnetization of about 2 to 10 gauss. Residence times of less than a minute were used. Magnetic separation is practical for separating small volumes of oily wastewater in which the major oil/water system present is secondary dispersions; energy requirements are large, and operational costs are high.

Thermal Separation

Separation of oil/water mixtures using thermal treatments is a feasible concept, but impractical if large volumes of wastewater are handled. However, thermal methods have been used to resolve emulsions present in oily wastewaters from crude oil production. After the emulsions are destabilized, oil can be separated from wastewater through use of other separation techniques. These methods have found only limited application and are adapted specifically for those wastewaters which contain mainly w/o emulsions or when water is present in small amounts. In systems such as these, the wastewater can be demulsified using thermal treatment. The process is economically attractive, if oil recovered from the wastewater has a high heating value or can be reprocessed and used as fuel oil. The major thermal treatment methods are heating, evaporation and distillation, and freezing or crystallization.

Heating--Heating has been used extensively to resolve crude oil emulsions. It has been used in conjunction with chemical addition to destabilize chemically stabilized emulsions. The process also increases the amount of dissolved oil in the wastewater. It is simple: the basic principle of this technique is alteration of the vapor pressure difference between oil and water. Energy requirements for large volumes of wastewater make this process uneconomical. Large equipment sizes are required, also.

Evaporation and Distillation--These separation techniques are similar to heating and suffer from the same disadvantages, even when the distillation process is carried out at reduced pressure. Complete separation of wastewater into distinct oil and water phases is impossible because, during operation, the oil fractionates and some fractions will be present in both condensate and distillate. Even when the distillation process is carried out in stages, there is a large energy demand for heating and providing reduced pressure before oil can be removed completely.

Freezing and Crystallization--In these methods, the difference in the freezing points of the two liquids is used to effect separation. Oil/water separation by freezing and crystallization is generally considered as economically infeasible when large volumes of wastewater are handled. Little literature on these techniques for oil/water separation is available. However, there is obvious need for complex refrigeration equipment and relatively large inputs of energy (Yu and Ventriglio, 1969).

Thus, thermal separation, though feasible, is not practical because of the high cost involved.

48

Sonic and Ultrasonic Separation

The use of sonic and ultrasonic devices to separate liquid/liquid mixtures is prevalent in the dairy industries, but the capability of these techniques to separate oil from oil/water mixtures has not been investigated fully. The lack of engineering assessment of these separation methods is a consequence of the use of sonic and ultrasonic devices, originally, in emulsification processes; they were deemed unsuitable for the reverse operation (demulsification). There are suggestions that these techniques may be feasible, if the appropriate wave frequency is used, for destabilizing emulsions. Destabilized emulsions can be coalesced and separated, using other separation techniques.

Determination of the appropriate wave frequencies necessary to destabilize emulsified oil/water systems is a costly operation. The characteristics of untreated wastewaters change and volumes of oily wastes to be processed are usually large. Using the wrong frequencies may break stable emulsions into finer dispersions or shatter already coalesced globules.

Coanda-Effect Separation

Separation of oil/water mixtures by utilizing the fluid-dynamic phenomenon called the "Coanda effect" is a new concept in liquid/liquid separation. The basic principle of this process was proposed by Henry Coanda, and the Navy has designed a separator capable of treating bilge and ballast wastewaters by the wall-attachment (Coanda-effect) phenomenon (Navy, 1974; Paszyc et al., 1975). In this process, an oil/water mixture is injected into an unbounded region. The jet splits into two subjets at the apex of concave walls; each subjet is deflected toward an adjacent wall, becomes attached, and flows along the wall enclosing a separation-bubble zone. The curved flow of each subjet creates a centrifugal force and the separation-bubble zone is formed. An oil droplet released at the jet nozzle experiences an inward motion due to the centrifugal force and undergoes radial displacement toward the bubble zone; it can coalesce with other oil droplets trapped there. Oil which accumulates in the bubble zone can be drawn off by suction. A schematic diagram of the process is shown in Figure 8.

Design--Important design parameters are: length of the attachment walls, radii of curvature of the splitting walls, velocity of fluid at the nozzle, and the size of the nozzle. Basically, a Coanda-effect separator comprises: inlet and outlet ports, an oil-collection chamber, oil/water interface detection probes, and an oil suction device. Multistage units are under design.

Performance--Results of test evaluations indicate that devices cannot achieve greater oil-removal efficiency than an API gravity separator or other primary separation technique. A major difficulty encountered with these devices is the turbulence that arises during processing, as a result of jet flow. Turbulence breaks oil dispersions into smaller droplets that are more difficult to separate. However, in the absence of turbulence, devices will be capable of separating only free oil and unstable primary dispersions. Oils with the same density as the aqueous phase will not be separated.

CLARIFIED
EFFLUENTS

REATTACHED JETS

VELOCITY
PROFILES

SPLITTER

SEPARATION
BUBBLE
ZONE

MIXTURE
JETS

OIL/WATER
MIXTURE
INLET

NOZZLE

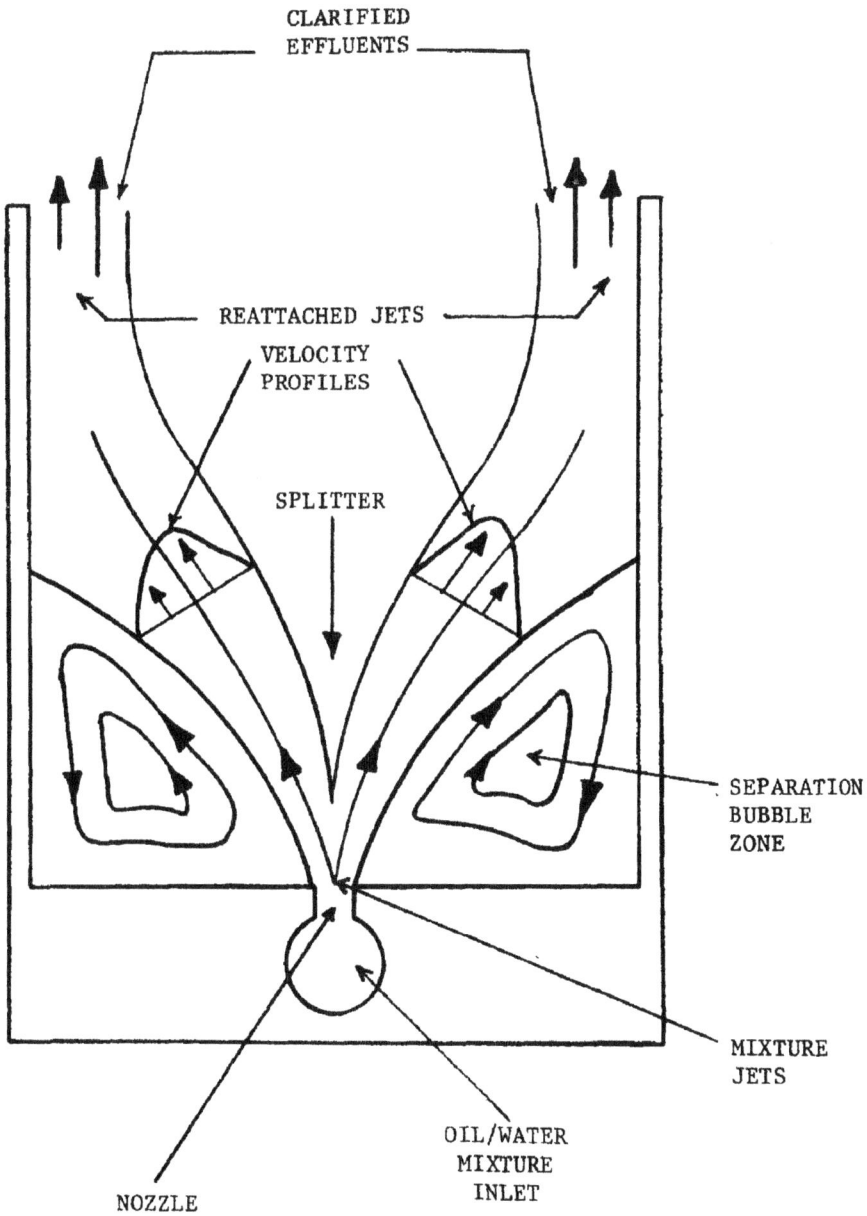

Figure 8.   Coanda-Effect Separator

50

Viscosity-Actuated Phase Separation

A new concept for separating a mixture of two immiscible liquids has been proposed and tested by Union Carbide Corporation. The principal driving force for the separation is the difference in viscosity of the liquids. The basic principle of this separation technique was proposed after laboratory observations of flow fields induced when a mixture of two immiscible liquids was subjected to pressure gradients. These laboratory tests revealed that if a drop of a mixture of oil and water is placed in the V-notch formed by two flat plates that can be squeezed together, separation of the liquids occurs because the low-viscosity water flows from the pressurized area more rapidly than the higher-viscosity oil (Union Carbide Corporation, 1973).

An apparatus was constructed to subject oil/water mixtures to the proper type of flow field in order to achieve separation of the mixture. The apparatus consists of a screw capable of rotating inside a threaded hollow cylinder. The rotor and stator are fitted so there is maximum eccentricity between the two parts during motion of the rotor. In operation, the changing clearance between the rotor and stator induces a squeezing action on oil/water mixtures and separation occurs.

Design--During a test evaluation, two types of viscosity-actuated phase separation devices were used. One unit (Orbiting Buttress Threaded Device) consists of an orbiting-screw rotor and a threaded hollow cylinder; both rotor and stator are constructed of rigid material. The second unit (Rotating Buttress Threaded Device) is similar to the first unit; however, the rotor is threaded and the stator is smooth. Later in the test evaluation, both units were constructed of an elastomeric material.

Important design parameters include the degree of eccentricity between the rotor and stator and the clearance between the two parts. Figure 9 is a diagram of an Orbiting Buttress Threaded Device.

Performance--Factors that influence device performance are separator geometry, the viscosity differential between the two liquids, and the balance between feed and separation rates. Results of test evaluations were not encouraging, and the poor performance reported was attributed to excessive clearances between the rotor and stator. For an effective separation, the oil-droplet size must be larger than the clearances between the stator and rotor. Because of geometric design limitations and inaccuracies in machining, the lower limit of the clearances could not be achieved. Results indicate that the devices increased emulsification instead of effecting separation. Some success was reported during separation of oil/water mixtures with oil as the continuous phase. These devices cannot qualify as oil/water separators, at present.

Chromatographic Separation

Chromatographic techniques are widely used in liquid/liquid separation and purification applications. Gas, liquid, and gel chromatographic methods have been suggested as processes capable of separating oil/water mixtures. However, there is no literature available on the use of these methods for

OIL/WATER MIXTURE INLET

ECCENTRIC
DRIVE SHAFT

OIL EFFLUENT

ORBITING
SHAFT

WATER
EFFLUENT

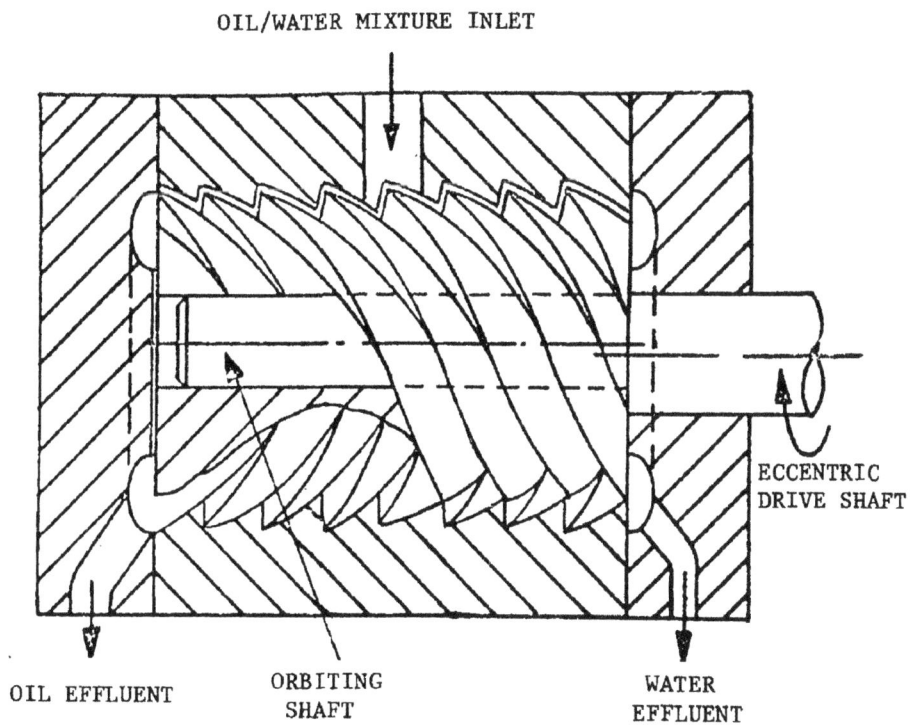

Figure 9. Orbiting Buttress Threaded Device

bulk oil/water separation (Yu and Ventriglio, 1969). Chromatography has use in several applications, but the technique suffers from the following disadvantages: small throughput, high head loss, and very low rates. Selection of column packings capable of extracting the oil phase from oil/water mixtures is difficult and expensive. Disposal of spent column materials is a problem and, if material is regenerated using an appropriate solvent, a secondary waste is generated. Therefore, the high cost of these methods has discouraged investigation as candidate oil/water separation processes.

Such sophisticated and costly separation methods may prove useful for small volumes of oily wastes containing little oil as regulations and discharge limits become more stringent.

SECTION 7

CRITICAL REVIEW OF SELECTED LITERATURE

Title: Coalescing Plates and Packs for Oil/Water Separation in Various
Shipboard Applications

Report No. and Date: CG-724305.2/6, January 1973

Authors: J. G. Merryman and E. R. Osterstock

Manufacturer of Equipment: General Electric Company, Philadelphia, Pa. 19101

Design Features: Device is a gravity-differential, parallel-plate
separator. Plates are convoluted and made of polypropylene. Plates are perforated, also, to enhance oil-globule coalescence. Equipment is divided into
four compartments; each compartment contains a plate pack.

Wastewater Characteristics: Four oils were used in the tests: (1)
Navy Special Fuel, (2) Navy Distillate Fuel, (3) Venezuelan Crude, and (4)
a mixture of hydraulic fluid and lubricating oil. Aqueous test fluids were:
(1) tap water and (2) seawater. Mixing of oil and water was accomplished by
three different methods, yielding different levels of emulsification. In the
first two methods, a Lightning mixer was operated at two speeds. In the
third method, oil and water were mixed and recirculated through a centrifugal
pump. Bilge water was simulated by adding detergent and sand to the oil/
water mixture containing test oil (4).

Methods of Analysis: Oil content of samples was measured by (1)
chloroform extraction and transmittance measurement in a B & L spectrophotom-
eter and (2) gravimetric analysis. All samples were acidified before analysis. Results of both analytical techniques were comparable. In most tests,
the colorimetric method was used, because of accuracy in the low concentration range.

Results: Several parameters that affect separation efficiency were
investigated. These parameters were plate length, oil concentration, temperature, and flow rate. Results showed the oil content of effluents was always
less than 50 ppm, for influent containing 500 ppm of oil. When influent oil
concentration was increased to 5000 ppm, effluent oil content was higher than
100 ppm. Effluents in tests using the centrifugal pump had more oil than
those produced in tests using the Lightning mixer. Addition of detergents
degraded device performance, also. Poor performance was observed when ship
motions were simulated by rocking the separator.

Critical Comments: Plate-type, gravity-differential separators cannot separate emulsions effectively. They are adequate for gross separation
only. Effluents from these devices have to be processed further to achieve
desired discharge quality.

Title: Feasibility Test Program of Application of Coalescing Phase Oil/Water
Separators to Self-compensating Fuel Tanks in Surface Ships

Report No. and Date: CG-D-88-74, May 1974

Authors: J. B. Arnaiz and E. Batutis

Manufacturer of Equipment: General Electric Company, Philadelphia, Pa. 19101

Design Features: Equipment is a commercial, parallel-plate-type,
gravity separator, capable of flow rates up to 1150 gpm. Length of the separator is 14 feet; plate length is 8 feet. This device has provision for
connecting the inlet to a ship fuel tank discharge port.

Wastewater Characteristics: Actual ballast water discharged from a
Navy oiler (U.S.S. Koelsh) during routine fueling operations. Ship had been
docked a few days.

Method of Analysis: During the test evaluation, on-line measurements
of entrained particle size and number were obtained for influent and effluent, using an HI-AC particle counter. On-line turbidity measurements were
made on the effluent, using a Keene turbidity meter. All samples were as-
sayed for oil content by carbon tetrachloride extraction and spectrophotometry. Prior to extraction, samples were acidified with a mixture of sulfuric and hydrochloric acids in a one-to-one ratio.

Results: Data reported by the performing agency were generally lower
than the results of chemical analyses of samples carried out by U.S. Navy
Laboratories. However, both sets of results indicate the oil content of
effluents was less than 8 ppm, in all tests. Influent oil concentration
varied from 4 to about 1000 ppm.

Critical Comments: Device functioned satisfactorily and separating
efficiency was unusually high. This may be the result of the absence of
emulsions in the oil/water mixture. Ship had been docked some time before
deballasting; it is conceivable that considerable separation had occurred
before the test evaluation was begun.

Title: Oil/Water Separator Evaluation

Report No. and Date: NCSL 252-75, July 1975

Author: John Mittleman

Manufacturer of Equipment: Assembled by author

Design Features: Device is a gravity-differential, plate-type separator. Plates are made of oleophilic material and arranged in stacks vertically in one chamber and horizontally in others. Equipment contains automatic valves, sensors, and other hardware items necessary for maintaining control of the movement of fluids in the system.

Wastewater Characteristics: In preliminary tests, synthetic wastewater was produced by emulsifying Navy Distillate Fuel Oil in tap water. Later, ballast and bilge water pumped from a naval vessel were used as feed.

Methods of Analysis: Two methods were used to quantify oil concentrations in samples: (1) visual quantification for those effluent samples in which there was a persistent sheen and (2) extractions with carbon tetrachloride followed by light-transmittance measurements at 420 nanometers.

Results: Data were presented graphically, and indicate poor performance throughout the test period. The oil content of all effluent samples averaged more than 50 ppm. Separated oil contained a high concentration of water, also. Device could not separate oil-coated solids.

Critical Comments: Gravity-differential separators are useful only for gross separations. Oily wastewater containing high oil concentration, as emulsions, cannot be separated in such devices. Results of this test evaluation are indicative of the limitations of plate-type oil/water separators.

Title: Vortex Concept for Separating Oil from Water

Report No. and Date: 4105.2/1, January 1973

Authors: R. C. Stoeffler and C. E. Jones

Manufacturer of Equipment: United Aircraft Corporation, East Hartford,
Conn. 06108

Design Features: Separators tested consist of 6-inch and 9.5-inch vortex tubes having four injection points; tubes were made of Lucite to allow visual inspection of operation; end walls were plain discs fastened to the vortex tube. A schematic diagram of the device is shown in Figure 10.

Wastewater Characteristics: Six types of oil (different densities and viscosities) were injected separately into the water feed line using a pressurized injection probe. In some tests, screens of different mesh sizes were inserted in the input line to emulsify the oil; in other tests, a centrifugal pump was used.

Method of Analysis: Oil content of samples was measured by carbon tetrachloride extraction and infrared analysis; values of the actual and measured oil concentrations were close.

Results: Overall, separator performance was poor. Oil content in

56

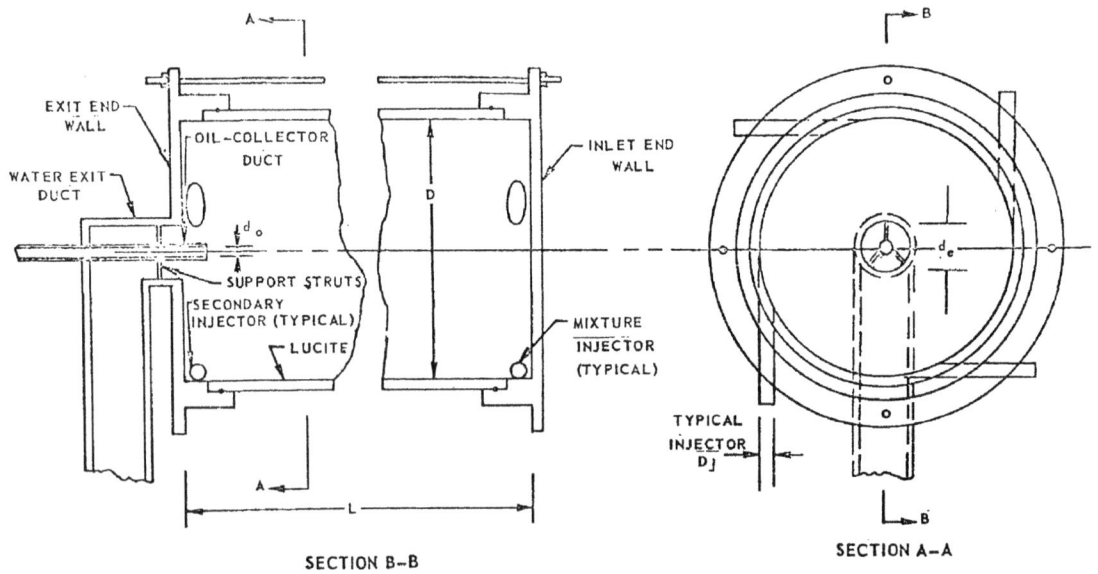

SECTION B-B

SECTION A-A

NOMINAL SEPARATOR CAPACITY, Q_M - GPM	DIMENSIONS				
	L – IN.	D – IN.	d_e – IN.	d_o –	D_j – IN.
10	18, 36	6	0.6, 1.2	0.18	0.209, 0.272, 0.323, 0.453
50	28.5, 57	9.5	0.95, 1.9	0.305	0.609, 0.718, 0.922

effluents was generally greater than 50 ppm; separated oil contained up to 95% water.

Critical Comments: Test data indicate the vortex concept is not feasible as an oil/water separation technique; the devices fail to meet stringent discharge limits. Separators were unable to separate emulsified oil; separated oil contained excessive free water, making reprocessing necessary. Slightly better separation was achieved when the process was followed by gravity separation.

Cost: The following prices were reported:
  100 gpm unit: $10,000
  1,000 " " : $94,000
  10,000 " " : $940,000

Title: Investigation of the Use of a Vortex Flow to Separate Oil from an Oil/Water Mixture

Report No. and Date: 714103/A/001, November 1970

Authors: A. E. Mensing, R. C. Stoeffler, W. R. Davison, and T. E. Hoover

Manufacturer of Equipment: United Aircraft Corporation, East Hartford, Conn. 06108

Design Features: Device is a 10-inch-diameter by 29.25-inch-long vortex tube; tube was made of Lucite to allow visual inspection; end walls were made of plain discs fastened directly to the tube. Injection points were located on the peripheral wall of the vortex tube.

Wastewater Characteristics: Influent oil/water mixtures were prepared by metering oil into a water line; four types of oil were used but none of the oils were emulsified.

Method of Analysis: Samples were left quiescent for several hours until the oil and water phases separated; then, the respective volumes of the two liquid phases were measured.

Results: Authors claim that it is possible to "capture" up to 85% of the injected oil and the separated oil can contain less than 15% water.

Critical Comments: The analytical method is unacceptable, because natural gravity separation is possible as the influent did not contain emulsified oil. Data presented graphically indicate overall performance was poor even when the process was followed by gravity separation. The authors' claims cannot be verified; thorough testing of the device is necessary and test data need to be reported in a better way before meaningful conclusions can be drawn.

Title: Vacuum Desorption Concept for Removing Oil from Water

Report No. and Data: USCG 734305.2/8, March 1973

Author: George M. Pomonik

Manufacturer of Equipment: Mechanics Research, Los Angeles, Calif. 90045

Design Features: System consists basically of: collection tank, vacuum separation tank, vacuum pump, revolving drum skimmer, and flow-control devices. A modification included polypropylene coalescing plates added to the vacuum tank.

Wastewater Characteristics: Mechanically emulsified oil/water mixtures were prepared with tap water and various oils. Occasionally, salt was added to simulate bilge and ballast water. A few tests were conducted with detergent and fine sand added to the influent. Mixing of oil and water was done by pump.

Method of Analysis: Oil content of samples was determined by extraction with petroleum ether, evaporation to dryness, and weighing of the residue.

Results: Oil concentration in effluents varied from 5 to 1000 ppm. Oil injected ahead of the main centrifugal pump could not be separated. The best effluents (5 and 7 ppm of oil) resulted when oil was added to tap water effluent from the main pump.

Critical Comments: This system is not suitable as a final oil/water separation device because of the poor performance. Improved design may enhance system capability for treating oil dispersions and suspended solids free of surface charges.

Title: Electrochemical Flotation Concept for Removing Oil from Water

Report No. and Date: USCG 734305.2/4, January 1973

Authors: Q. H. McKenna, H. Helber, L. M. Carrell, and R. F. Tobias

Manufacturer of Equipment: Lockheed Aircraft Service Company, Ontario, Calif. 91761

Design Features: The system consists of a rectangular flotation cell, approximately 4 feet long, constructed from glass-reinforced polyester. The cathode is stainless steel mesh. The anode is made from fine platinum-10% iridium alloy wire, spot-welded to a columbian substrate.

Wastewater Characteristics: Simulated bilge and ballast waters using a combination of tap water, sea salts, and different oils were tested. Emulsification involved blending the mixture with a Lightning mixer for 5 minutes before feeding, by gravity, to a high shear pump operating at 500 psig.

Stability tests indicated that the mixtures contained unstable emulsions after they were prepared. Oil concentrations in the aqueous phases dropped to about 100 ppm from higher initial concentrations after a few hours.

Methods of Analysis: Two methods were used for analyzing samples. One method involved extraction with solvent, followed by UV analysis. Solvent was a mixture of the following components: 60% 2-propanol, 10% petroleum ether, 20% seawater, and 10% tap water. In the second method, pure ether was used as the extracting solvent. Oil concentrations determined by both methods were similar.

Results: Experimental data indicate the oil concentration of all effluents was lower than 20 ppm, for influents containing oil concentrations of 3000 to 4000 ppm.

Critical Comments: If developed adequately, the electrochemical flotation concept can separate oil from water effectively. The oil/water systems most susceptible to separation will be oil dispersions and suspended solids stabilized by surface charges. Consistent effluent quality of less than 10 ppm of oil can be achieved. The system was not tested thoroughly for the effects of variable oil concentration in the influent. Simulated ship motion did not degrade system performance. Cell volume is large and the cost of chemicals and equipment is very high. Problems encountered in the process are: (1) production of chlorine gas which dissolves in the effluent, to a concentration of 250 ppm—concentration is beyond the allowable discharge level for chlorine, making further treatment a necessity; (2) production of hydrogen gas, causing a fire hazard; and (3) temperature elevation of effluent, due to ohmic heating of the electrodes, leading to thermal pollution and energy wastage.

Cost: 10 gpm unit: $10,000
        100 "   " : $80,500
       1000 "   " : $600,000

Title: Separation of Oil in Bilge Water by Semipermeable Membrane

Report No. and Date: AD-A023-289, May 1971

Authors: W. L. Adamson and M. W. Titus

Manufacturer of Equipment: Bench-scale apparatus assembled by authors

Design Features: Device consists of a 3-inch-inside-diameter, stainless steel cylinder in which was mounted the cellulose-acetate membrane (Eastman Chemical type HF). The membrane was placed on a porous stainless steel disk supported on a perforated metal disk. Operating pressures ranged from 550 to 675 psig.

Wastewater Characteristics: The feed solution was prepared from distilled water and 2190-TEP lubricating oil. The oil/water solution was stirred mechanically for 1 hour, in a mixing tank, and gravity-fed to a reciprocating pump. A magnetic stirrer located at the feed inlet provided further emulsification of the feed.

Method of Analysis: All samples were analyzed for oil content using carbon tetrachloride extraction and infrared absorbance measurement. Two extractions with carbon tetrachloride were made: 25 ml of CCl_4 in the first, and 15 ml of CCl_4 in the second.

Results: The average oil content of all effluent samples was below 25 ppm of oil with feed containing up to 10,000 ppm of oil. The longest run lasted for about 15 hours.

Critical Comments: This test evaluation shows the feasibility of using cellulose-acetate membranes for separating oil/water mixtures. The device was not tested in detail, because the feed wastewater characteristics were different from those of bilge and ballast water or petrochemical waste-waters. There was a sharp decline in permeate flow rate with increasing operating time, indicating that fouling of the membrane may have occurred. Repeated cleaning with trichloroethylene partially restored permeate flow rate.

Title: Study of Hydrophilic Membranes for Oil-Water Separation

Report No. and Date: 4305.2/7, January 1973

Authors: C. E. Milstead and J. F. Loos

Manufacturer of Equipment: Gulf Environmental Systems Company, P. O. Box 81608, San Diego, Calif. 81608

Design Features: Twenty membrane materials were evaluated as candidates for use in ultrafiltration. Hydrolyzed asymmetric cellulose-acetate was selected, and tests were conducted with this membrane in a spiral-wound configuration.

Wastewater Characteristics: Four different oils were used: Gulf Harmony lubricating oil, diesel fuel, a California crude oil, and actual bilge water from a U.S. Navy ship (U.S.S. Monticello) that had been in harbor for 2 weeks. Oil/water mixtures were prepared in a feed reservoir by a mixing pump, with tap water and oil.

Methods of Analysis: Oil content of samples was determined using an extraction-gravimetric technique and Total Carbon Analysis. The precision of the extraction-gravimetric technique, based on data, was better than ±5% for lubricating oil/water mixtures but large errors were encountered with crude oil/water mixtures.

Results: Test results indicate the following:

a) Oil content of effluents averaged 1.3 ppm with feeds containing up to 50,000 ppm of lube oil; 2.4, 5 and 1.5 ppm with feeds containing 2,500

61

ppm of crude oil, 2,500 ppm of diesel oil, and actual bilge water, respectively.

b) Oil content of effluent reached a maximum of 18 ppm with feeds containing 10,000 ppm of diesel oil.

Critical Comments: The surface-hydrolyzed cellulose-acetate membrane performed satisfactorily in all tests and can produce effluents that contain less than 10 ppm of oil. Variations of operating conditions did not affect device performance adversely. Membrane fouling is a problem, and an adequate cleaning method to restore product flux is lacking. For consistent performance, feed should be free of suspended solids.

Cost: The estimated costs of two units are as follows: 100 gpm unit: $27,000; 1000 gpm unit: $245,000.

Title: Ultrafiltration Concept for Separating Oil from Water

Report No. and Date: 734305.2/2, January 1973

Authors: R. L. Goldsmith and S. Hossain

Manufacturer of Equipment: Abcor, Inc., 341 Vassar Street, Cambridge, Mass. 02139

Design Features: Ultrafiltration membranes tested were (1) moderately hydrophilic cellulose-acetate and (2) highly hydrophilic cellulose-acetate. Both were studied in a tubular configuration; each tube had an internal diameter of 1 inch and membrane pore sizes were less than $0.01~\mu$. Ultrafiltration rates were high, generally in the range 25-150 gal/day/sq ft.

Wastewater Characteristics: The oils tested were No. 6 fuel oil, a Venezuelan crude, lubricating oil, and kerosene. Very unstable emulsions were obtained by gravity feeding these oils into recirculated tap water.

Methods of Analysis: The analytical methods used were:

a) Gravimetric--samples were acidified with sulfuric acid and oil in the samples was extracted with petroleum ether; extract was dried and the residue from the drying step was weighed.
b) Infrared spectrophotometry following extraction with carbon tetrachloride.
c) UV spectrophotometry following extraction with carbon tetrachloride. Method (b) was the least sensitive. Samples were kept refrigerated (35°F) for 1 to 5 days before analysis.

Results: The authors claim that, at oil input ratios of up to 90%, effluents were uniformly free of visible oil and had less than 10 ppm of oil. All effluents were reported to be completely free of turbidity and floating oil sheen, and were crystal-clear. However, a very faint oil odor and taste were generally detectable.

Critical Comments: Test results from the gravimetric and infrared spectrophotometric techniques were quite dissimilar. Most analyses were by the gravimetric technique, which is very sensitive to drying temperature. Test results cannot be entirely correct. The presence of oil odor and taste indicate that dissolved oil passed the membrane, and the concentration of dissolved oil could be far greater than the 10 ppm reported for all effluents. Test data were not properly reported, and further testing is necessary before meaningful conclusions can be made. Membrane fouling is a problem.

Title: Oil-Water Separation with Noncellulosic Ultrafiltration Systems

Report No. and Date: Proceedings of Joint Conference on Prevention and Control of Oil Spills, 1975, pp. 443-447

Authors: P. Schatzberg, L. R. Harris, C. M. Adema, D. F. Jackson, and C. M. Kelly

Manufacturer of Equipment: Laboratory models were assembled by authors

Design Features: Four different modules were tested:

a) A tubular module consisted of a bundle of porous carbon tubes, each having an internal diameter of 0.25 inch and a length of 40 inches; the membrane had an apparent pore diameter of 20 Å.

b) Hollow-fiber modules, in two configurations, were used. One consisted of a bundle of hollow fibers having an internal diameter of 0.017 inch and a length of 24 inches; this system could be backflushed, and total effective membrane surface area was 25 sq ft; the membrane had an apparent pore diameter of 38 Å and a nominal molecular weight cutoff of 10,000. In the second configuration, the internal diameter of fibers was 0.020 inch and the effective membrane area of the bundle was 30 sq ft; the nominal molecular weight cutoff was 80,000 and the apparent pore diameter was 100 Å.

c) The spiral-wound module consisted of a series of membrane sheets, separated by corrugated spacers and combined in a spiral-wound cylindrical shape; total membrane area was 35 sq ft and pore diameter was approximately 50 Å. The membrane's nominal molecular weight cutoff was 5,000 to 10,000.

d) A plate and frame configuration consisted of a series of membrane sheets separated by fine fiber cloths; the membrane had an effective area of 5 sq ft and an apparent pore diameter of approximately 40 Å. The membrane's nominal molecular weight cutoff was 100,000.

Wastewater Characteristics: Two types of oil-in-water emulsions were prepared, using a lubricating oil and fresh water. Initially a high-speed blender was used to mix the oil and water; later, stabler emulsions were prepared using an ultrasonic mixer.

Method of Analysis: Oil-in-water analyses were made by infrared spectrophotometry, following carbon tetrachloride extraction.

Results: Each of the non-cellulosic membranes investigated demonstrated a capacity to separate emulsified and suspended oil from water. All but the tubular modules consistently produced effluents containing less than 15 ppm of oil.

Critical Comments: All modules tested gave satisfactory performance. The major problem encountered was a decline of flux rate as testing progressed. Therefore, permeate flushing and backwashing with detergent were necessary. However, complete recovery of flux rate could not be obtained with any of the non-cellulosic membranes. Despite the good separation reported, it is doubtful if these devices are capable of separating dissolved oil or emulsified oil much smaller than the membrane pore diameter.

Title: Development of a Coalescing Type Oil/Water Separator for Marine Service

Report No. and Date: Aqua-Chem Technical Report presented at SNAME Meeting, San Diego, Calif., February 18, 1970

Authors: Lee J. Hartenstein and Thomas E. Lindemuth

Manufacturer of Equipment: Aqua-Chem, Inc., Waukesha, Wis.

Design Features: Device has three stages. The first stage is a screen; three cartridge-type coalescer elements are present in the second and third stages. Removal of oil in all stages is controlled by capacitance-type oil/water interface detectors. Each chamber is equipped with electrical heaters to reduce oil viscosity and to drive off small amounts of oil entrained in the separated water phase.

Wastewater Characteristics: Oil is fed into circulating fresh water (occasionally seawater) at the suction or discharge port of a centrifugal pump to produce differing emulsified oil/water mixtures.

Method of Analysis: Technique(s) used in analyzing samples for oil content not stated.

Results: Data were presented graphically and indicate effluent oil concentrations were below 80 ppm, with influents containing 10% oil.

Critical Comments: Since analytical methods were not stated, data reported lacked credibility; the operating temperature is high and may alter solubility of oil in the treated aqueous phase.

Title: Oily Water Separator: Liquid-Liquid Separation by a Commercial Self-cleaning Edge Filter

Report No. and Date: COM-71-01095, January 19, 1971

Author: J. R. Hefler

Manufacturer of Equipment: AMF Beaird, Inc., Uncasville, Conn. 06382

Design Features: The system consists of a tank with internal baffles and tangential inlets. Cartridge-type filter elements having spacings of 0.0015 inch were designed by Cuno Engineering Corporation. Filter elements can be cleaned continuously by cartridge rotation. Automatic oil detection probes provide recirculation of effluent for reprocessing, if oil concentration is high.

Wastewater Characteristics: Seawater and three grades of Bunker C oil, of different densities, were used as test fluids. The oils were injected upstream and downstream of a 3450-rpm centrifugal pump, into seawater, to provide the wastewater feed.

Method of Analysis: Samples are mixed with "sufficient" chloroform and evaporated to dryness at 75°C; the weight fraction of oil present in a sample is determined.

Results: Effluents contained as much as 2000 ppm oil. Separation efficiency was poor. Oil with specific gravity close to that of seawater could not be separated.

Critical Comments: Device was poorly designed and separation was not possible when oil was injected ahead of the pump. Oil dispersions with droplet sizes less than 0.002-inch diameter were not separated. Test results cannot be correlated, due to the poor experimental techniques used.

Title: Experimental Evaluation of Fibrous Bed Coalescers for Separating Oil-Water Emulsions

Report No. and Date: EPA Project No. 12050DRC, November 1971

Authors: W. M. Langdon and D. T. Wasan

Manufacturer of Equipment: Illinois Institute of Technology, Chicago, Ill. 60616

Design Features: Device is a 1-sq ft coalescer unit built into a filter press framework. The coalescer unit is made of fiberglass filaments, 3.2 μ in diameter, coated with isobutyl methacrylate resin for stability.

Wastewater Characteristics: Tap water and a mixture of 50% kerosene and 50% pollutant material from treated hot mill cooling water (similar to No. 30 lube oil) were agitated and recycled through a 3450-rpm centrifugal pump for 1 hour. Primary and secondary dispersions of the oils in water were produced.

Methods of Analysis: Oil concentrations in samples were determined by light transmission and Hach turbidimeter measurements. Tabulated data, on samples analyzed by both methods, were not converted to parts per million for comparison.

Results: Oil-separation efficiency varied from 70 to 99%, at influent oil concentrations of 50 to 500 ppm. Higher efficiences were reported for fibers coated with resins than for uncoated fibers.

Critical Comments: The analytical methods used do not detect dissolved oil, which may have been appreciable. Therefore, oil concentrations in effluents are higher than reported. Abrupt increases of oil in effluent occurred if runs were not continuous; feed pretreatment is required to control the large pressure drops encountered and to prolong fiber life.

Cost: Equipment cost was not specified; operating costs are estimated at $0.13/$10^3$/gal for single-fiber use and $0.01/$10^3$/gal if fibers can be regenerated.

Title: Oily Water Separation System

Report No. and Date: COM-72-10561, January 1972

Author: R. J. Skocypec

Manufacturer of Equipment: Esso Research and Engineering Department, Linden, N. J. 07036

Design Features: Separator consists of a coalescing element upstream of a settling chamber. There is an AMF-Cuno Super Auto-Klean Filter upstream of the device.

Wastewater Characteristics: Shoreside tests were performed with ballast water discharged from ships.

Method of Analysis: All samples were analyzed for oil content using an infrared absorption technique.

Results: Average oil-removal efficiencies reported range from less than 5 to nearly 90%.

Critical Comments: The coalescer was easily plugged and device was not tested sufficiently. Performance was poor and the test procedure was inadequate.

Title: Test and Evaluation of a 50-Gallon-per-Minute Oil/Water Separator

Report No. and Date: AD 785-223, July 1972

Author: E. C. Russell

Manufacturer of Equipment: Separations and Recovery Systems, Inc., Santa Ana, Calif. 92705

Design Features: The SRS separator consists of two, skid-mounted,

16-inch-in-diameter by 47-inch-long high-pressure vessels, connected in series. Each vessel contains three 6-inch-in-diameter and 22-inch-long coalescer elements, mounted in parallel. The device is equipped with a supply pump and a capacitance-type probe that controls the automatic oil-discharge cycle of the system.

Wastewater Characteristics: Various quantities of differing oils were metered into recirculating fresh water, at the suction side of a pump, to produce an emulsified oil/water mixture. In some test runs, dry sand was added to the oil/water mixture.

Methods of Analysis: Three methods were used for determining the oil content of samples: (1) turbidity, (2) visual inspection, and (3) CCl4 extraction and infrared spectrophotometry.

Results: Data from the turbidity meter measurements indicate oil concentrations in effluents were below 60 ppm, but values reported for infrared analyses were as high as 141 ppm.

Critical Comments: The objective of these tests was no visible "sheen" in discharged waters, which device easily achieved. Analytical results from the three methods were not similar.

Title: Test and Evaluation of Oil-Water Separation Systems

Report No. and Date: CR 73.015, November 8, 1972

Author: A. V. Sims

Manufacturer of Equipment: The devices tested are (1) Fram Corporation separator and (2) Separation and Recovery Systems separator

Design Features: The Fram separator consists of a preconditioning unit (filter cartridge with 25-μ pore size), a gravity separation stage, and a coalescing stage (5-μ pore size filter cartridge). Device is equipped with an interface controller and a manually operated oil valve. The SRS separator has a prefilter (25-μ pore size) and two stages of coalescing filters (5-μ pore size); device is equipped with an interface controller, and oil and water control valves.

Wastewater Characteristics: Various quantities of Navy Special Fuel Oil were intimately mixed with seawater by a centrifugal pump. Feed mixtures contained mechanically emulsified oil.

Method of Analysis: Oil in samples was extracted by chloroform (three separate extractions) and analyzed by infrared spectrophotometry. The report states: "At concentrations less than 10 ppm, the average analytical accuracy was about 20%."

Results: The average oil content of effluents from the Fram separator was less than 3 ppm, with influents containing 200 ppm oil. The average oil content of effluents from the SRS separator was less than 1 ppm, with influents containing 350 ppm oil.

Critical Comments: Oil-recovery efficiencies higher than 95% are reported. However, devices were not tested adequately; stability of feed mixtures was not evaluated. Additional tests performed on a combined unit, which included the SRS separator, showed 100% oil-removal efficiency.

Title: Test and Evaluation of Oil Pollution Abatement Devices for Shipboard Use: Phase I

Report No. and Date: AD-762-498, March 1972

Authors: L. B. Norton and F. Perrini

Manufacturer of Equipment: Not stated

Design Features: Several separators were tested:

Separator A: a two-stage vertical filter/coalescer unit equipped with a 3450-rpm centrifugal pump

Separator B: a four-stage horizontal filter/coalescer unit equipped with a centrifugal pump

Separator C: a three-stage (prefilter, gravity, and coalescing) unit equipped with a double diaphragm pump

Separator D: a two-stage (gravity and coalescing) unit equipped with a centrifugal pump

Separator E: a three-stage (two gravity sections and a coalescer/ absorber stage) unit equipped with a centrifugal pump

Separator F: prefilter, twin automatic vortex dirt separators, a gravity stage, and four carbon coalescing stages; device is equipped with a low-shear pump

Wastewater Characteristics: Oil/water mixtures of No. 2 fuel oil and tap water were used as feed. Emulsification of feed was produced by the pump with which device is equipped.

Methods of Analysis: Oil content of samples was measured by (1) turbidity meter, (2) gravimetric analysis, (3) Total Organic Carbon analysis, (4) electronic microbalance, and (5) visual inspection.

Results: Most effluents contained visible oil "sheens."

Critical Comments: Report does not contain any useful information; numerical data on oil content of effluents are not given. Evaluation procedures appear inadequate, and report is not coherent.

Title: Analytical Examination of Oil/Water Separation by Coalescence

Report No. and Date: Control Technology R&D, pp. 403-408 (USEPA)

Authors: S. M. Finger and T. S. Yu

Manufacturer of Equipment: Laboratory prototype

Design Features: System is a three-stage separation device: the first stage is a cylindrical gravity separator; the second stage contains a prefilter; the third stage is the coalescer filter. Coalescer elements used were of the cylindrical cartridge type, made of resin-coated fiberglass covered with cotton socks. Four-inch-diameter elements were positioned horizontally in a glass chamber, allowing for visual inspection of element performance.

Wastewater Characteristics: The influent oil/water mixture to the system was prepared by metering oil and water through a centrifugal pump. Severn River water was used, and the oils were Navy Distillate Fuel Oil and MS-2190-TEP lubricating oil; the shearing action of the pump effectively mixed the oil and water.

Method of Analysis: Samples were analyzed for oil content by extraction with carbon tetrachloride followed by infrared absorbance measurements.

Results: Under most conditions studied, effluent water contained less than 15 ppm oil. Only 10% of the samples analyzed contained oil more than this amount.

Critical Comments: System was adequately tested for the effects of several parameters on performance. Report is well written; however, stability analyses of feed streams should have been performed.

Title: Technologies for Shipboard Oil Pollution Abatement: Effects of Operational Parameters on Coalescence

Report No. and Date: 3598, August 1972

Authors: S. M. Finger and T. S. Yu

Manufacturer of Equipment: Naval Ship Research and Developmental Center, Bethesda, Md. 20034

Design Features: System is a three-stage separator; cartridge-type coalescer elements were made of resin-coated glass fibers. The first stage is empty, acting as a conventional gravity separator; the second stage is a prefilter; and the third stage contains the coalescer elements.

Wastewater Characteristics: Oils were metered into recirculating river water at the suction side of a centrifugal pump, producing mechanically emulsified oil/water mixtures.

Method of Analysis: An infrared spectrophotometric analysis developed at the Naval Shipyard Laboratory (methodology was not stated) was used to detect oil content of samples.

Results: Authors state that 60 out of 66 samples analyzed for oil content contained less than 15 ppm oil; influent oil concentrations were not stated.

Critical Comments: Test objective was to determine the effects of some operational parameters on a coalescence device; the report states that dirt, silt, and highly viscous oils can clog filter elements. The credibility of test results cannot be confirmed because the analytical technique used was not stated in the report.

Title: Test and Evaluation of Oil Pollution Abatement Devices for Shipboard Use: Phase II

Report No. and Date: AD 762-499, September 1972

Author: L. B. Norton

Manufacturer of Equipment: Not stated

Design Features: Three different separators were tested:

Separator A: a two-stage vertical filter/coalescer unit, containing automatic oil-discharge control valves; a prefilter was not provided.

Separator B: a larger version of separator A, but contains a prefilter.

Separator C: a three-stage filter/ coalescer/gravity unit; this device has automatic and manual oil-discharge valves

Wastewater Characteristics: Oil and solids were injected in fresh water circulating through three different pumps: centrifugal, vane, and double diaphragm. Oil/water mixtures produced contained emulsified oil.

Methods of Analysis: The oil content of samples was determined by two methods: (1) turbidity and (2) visual observation.

Results: Most effluents had "no visible sheen." Occasionally separation performance was poor; substitution of vane pumps for the system's centrifugal pumps did not improve performance. Water content of separated oils was high.

Critical Comments: Analytical methods did not give a true indication of the oil content of samples. Tests were not complete and the report is poorly organized.

Title: Test and Evaluation of Oil Pollution Abatement Devices for Shipboard Use: Phase III--Final

Report No. and Date: AD 762-488, January 1973

Author: L. B. Norton

Manufacturer of Equipment: Omitted

Design Features: Device is a two-staged unit, consisting of a pre-filter made of 10-μ-pore-size elements and 10 pleated paper cartridges, and a second stage containing 5 cartridge filter elements. Equipment has oil/water interface probes and discharge valves.

Wastewater Characteristics: Device was installed on a U.S. Coast ' Guard cutter to process feed streams of actual bilge and ballast waters.

Methods of Analysis: Samples were analyzed by (1) microbalance and (2) Total Organic Carbon measurements.

Results: Data were not stated. The average oil content of the effluent, in one run, was reported to be 28 ppm; oily effluents generally contained some entrained water. The author claims that overall separator performance was acceptable.

Critical Comments: The report is badly written. The device was not tested sufficiently; it is impossible to draw conclusions from reported data. Analytical techniques are vague. Device was susceptible to dirt loading.

Title: Separation of Oil Dispersions from Water by Fibrous Bed Coalescers

Report No. and Date: Environ. Sci. Technol., 6, No. 10, 907 (October 1972)

Authors: W. M. Langdon, P. P. Naik, and D. T. Wasan

Manufacturer of Equipment: Illinois Institute of Technology, Chicago, Ill. 60616

Design Features: Device is constructed of aluminum and consists of two types of fibers (Owens Corning glass fiber having 3.2-μ diameter and Owens Corning Aerocor coarse glass fiber of 10.1-μ diameter). Glass fiber mats are clamped between perforated plates; 100-mesh Monel screens, coated with TFE, precede the coalescer/filter elements.

Wastewater Characteristics: Standardized oil/water mixtures were prepared by metering oil into tap water, circulating through a ring pump operating at 3450 rpm. Pollutant oil from a skimming tank at Interlake Steel Corporation and Interlake Steel Corporation No. 30 grade automotive lubrication oil were used.

Method of Analysis: Oil concentrations in influent and effluent streams were determined by light transmission.

Results: Oil content of effluents varied from 7 ppm to generally non-detectable, with influent oil concentrations of 50 to 500 ppm.

Critical Comments: It is doubtful that light transmission can detect oil in the range 0-50 ppm with accuracy. Since this method was used in analyzing product samples, the reported efficiency of separation is probably erroneous.

Title: RPC Division, Midland-Ross Corporation 10-Gallon-per-Minute Liquid/ Liquid Separator

Report No. and Date: 2058, May 1973

Author: E. C. Russell

Manufacturer of Equipment: RPC Division, Midland-Moss Corporation, Roxboro, N. C. 27573

Design Features: This is a three-stage coalescence-type device. A cylindrical, horizontal tank, 70 inches long and 12 inches in diameter houses the coalescer elements. The first-stage element is 12 inches long and 10 inches in diameter; in the second and third stages, cartridge elements are 6 inches long and 10 inches in diameter.

Wastewater Characteristics: Quantities of differing oils were metered into circulating, prefiltered fresh water, at the suction side of a supply pump, to produce mechanically emulsified oil/water mixtures.

Methods of Analysis: Four methods were used for analyzing samples: (1) on-line ultraviolet energy absorption, (2) on-line fluorescence detection, (3) turbidity, and (4) Total Organic Carbon (TOC) analysis. Oil concentrations determined by the different methods were not similar.

Results: Data from TOC analysis indicate oil concentrations in effluents were below 10 ppm, with influents containing up to 32% oil. Other analytical methods gave much higher values (200 ppm), with influents containing 3% oil.

Critical Comments: Pressure drops in this equipment were high after short operating times, indicating the device can be easily plugged. The objective of the test evaluation, i.e. "no visible sheen" in effluents, was met despite the dissimilarity in the data reported for the various analytical methods.

Title: Fram Corporation Model OWS-23-FCI-USCG Oil/Water Separator

Report No. and Date: 2059, May 1973

Author: E. C. Russell

Manufacturer of Equipment: Fram Corporation, Tulsa, Okla. 74160

Design Features: A multistage, skid-mounted device equipped with a double-diaphragm pneumatic supply pump. The first stage is a preconditioner; the second stage is an inclined-plate, gravity separator; the last stage contains a cartridge-type coalescer element.

Wastewater Characteristics: Test fluid was prefiltered tap water. Various oils were used to produce oil/water mixtures. The shearing action of a pump emulsified the mixture.

Methods of Analysis: Three methods were used for analyzing samples: (1) on-line fluorescence detection, (2) turbidity, and (3) Total Organic Carbon (TOC) analyses. Oil concentrations determined by the different methods were not similar.

Results: TOC analyses indicate an average oil concentration of 25 ppm in effluents, with influents having up to 9% oil. Concentrations obtained by on-line fluorescence detection were higher.

Critical Comments: Device was not thoroughly tested; however, performance was poor. System is not capable of treating slightly stable emulsions.

Title: Separation and Recovery Systems, Inc. 100-Gallon-per-Minute Oil/Water Separator

Report No. and Date: 2060, May 1973

Author: E. C. Russell

Manufacturer of Equipment: Separation and Recovery Systems, Inc., Santa Ana, Calif. 92705

Design Features: Device is comprised of the following: prefilter; two skid-mounted (20-inch diameter by 60-inch diameter by 60 inches long) high-pressure vessels, connected in series; high-shear supply pump; control valves, etc. Each vessel contains five (6-inch diameter by 22 inches long) cartridge-type filter elements, mounted in parallel.

Wastewater Characteristics: Various types of contaminant oils were mixed with prefiltered fresh water and synthetic seawater to produce oil/ water mixtures. Dry fine sand was added occasionally. The shear of the supply pump emulsified the mixtures.

Methods of Analysis: Two methods were used for analyzing samples: (1) on-line turbidity measurements and (2) crystal microbalance.

Results: Data from turbidity measurements indicated acceptable performance, but concentrations reported from the crystal microbalance technique were much higher; oil concentrations in effluents averaged 35 ppm.

Critical Comments: Device performance met the test objective of "no visible sheen" in discharge waters. The analytical techniques used provide only rough estimates of oil content in effluent samples tested, and performance efficiency cannot be determined accurately.

Title: Oil/Water Pollution Program: Phase I

Report No. and Date: NAPTC-PE-27, July 1973

Authors: A. P. Pontello, F. G. Woessner, and R. J. Delfosse

Manufacturer of Equipment: Velcon Corporation

Design Features: System consists of an experimental coalescer/filter element, approximately 20 inches long and 3.75 inches in diameter (Velcon TE 3-27), installed vertically in a cylindrical vessel.

Wastewater Characteristics: Navy Distillate Fuel Oil was injected into circulating tap water at the suction end of a vane pump. Primary and secondary dispersions (emulsions) were produced by pump shearing forces.

Methods of Analysis: Oil concentrations in samples were measured by two methods: (1) turbidimetry and (2) carbon tetrachloride extractions and infrared spectrophotometry.

Results: Data were not tabulated. The authors claim that 4 ppm of oil was present in the effluent, when the influent contained 100 ppm oil.

Critical Comments: Stability tests were not performed on wastewater; the oily wastewater used was not representative of bilge or ballast water. Tests conducted on the device were limited; throughput was small because of excessive differential pressure on the system.

Title: Oil/Water Pollution Program: Phase II

Report No. and Data: AD-A009-093, October 1974

Authors: A. P. Pontello, C. J. Collick, J. J. Palmer, and A. J. Rollo

Manufacturer of Equipment: Several manufacturers of coalescer elements

Design Features: Details of the different coalescer elements are as follows:

    a) FRAM PC-11: element is 14.5 inches long and 3.5 inches in diameter; made of fiberglass, pleated paper, and perforated screen frames; flow is inside-out.

    b) Velcon Corporation: coalescer element is 20 inches long and 1.25 inches in diameter; consists of various layers of fiberglass sandwiched between a metal screen and encased in a cylindrical vessel made of synthetic material.

c) Keene Corporation: element is 20 inches long and 1.25 inches in diameter; made of variable density fiberglass layers, plastic-coated mesh screen, a pleated paper core, and a perforated metal screen.

d) SRS: element has dimensions similar to the Keene model but consists of fiberglass, cloth, and two types of plastic-coated mesh.

e) Bendix: element has the same dimensions as the Keene coalescer but consists of two fiberglass materials of different density.

Wastewater Characteristics: Navy Distillate Fuel Oil was injected at the suction side of a centrifugal pump circulating tap water; the resulting emulsified oil/water mixture was used as test fluid. Detergents were used, also.

Methods of Analysis: Four methods were used to analyze samples: (1) samples were rated by visual inspection (method is subjective), (2) turbidity measurements, (3) CCl_4 extraction and infrared spectrophotometry, and (4) estimation of sheen on water surfaces (sheen index).

Results: Oil concentration in influents was varied from 100 to 50,000 ppm; the testing process was not systematic, so that data obtained on various coalescers could not be compared.

Velcon: oil concentration in effluents averaged 5 ppm; free water was present in coalesced oil and the quantity of free water increased with throughput; differential pressure in the system reached 28.7 psi after 25 hours of operation.

Keene: oil concentration in effluents averaged 4 ppm, without detergents; performance was unsatisfactory when detergent was present in the wastewater.

Fram: effluents contained 2 ppm oil, when coalescer was operated with a prefilter; without a prefilter, oil concentration in effluents reached 17 ppm.

SRS: in the absence of detergents, effluents contained an average of 2 ppm oil; with detergents, oil concentration in effluents rose to 6.5 ppm. Free water (20 ppm) was present in coalesced oil.

Critical Comments: Stability tests performed on the process streams indicate that the oil/water mixtures treated were very unstable; separation of oil (when the mixtures were left undisturbed) was 40 to 80% complete. Test procedures were not varied, and some of the data obtained were meaningless. Analytical methods are suspect.

Title: Development of a Batchwise In-Situ Regeneration-Type Separator to Remove Oil from Oil-Water Suspensions

Report No. and Date: Technical Report 7080-3, December 1974

Author: D. H. Fruman

Manufacturer of Equipment: Hydronautics, Inc., Laurel, Md. 20810

Design Features: System (HOWS Model 0-600) is a completely self-contained, fully automated module, capable of treating up to 600 gpm of oily wastewater. Device consists of a three-compartment chamber, made up of an upstream header, a middle filtration section containing the filtering material between two perforated plates (one fixed and the other free to move), and a downstream decanter header containing an inclined plate. Filter material is a thick, open-reticulated, oleophilic foam which is regenerated by squeezing with the movable perforated plate.

Wastewater Characteristics: Tests were conducted at the Navy Fuel Reclamation Plant in Virginia: influents were taken from the middle chamber of a primary gravity separator and from storage tanks used for ballast and bilge waters discharged from Navy ships.

Method of Analysis: Samples were analyzed by light transmission measurements. Some samples were analyzed for oil content by the Naval Systems Research and Development Laboratory, Annapolis; technique was not stated.

Results: Oil content of separated water was high; oil-removal efficiency was poor. Oil content of effluents was generally higher than 40 ppm, with influents containing up to 300 ppm oil.

Critical Comments: System is suitable for gross oil/water separation; efficiency is comparable to that of ordinary gravity separators. Aging of foam leads to poor performance; high cost of system may discourage use.

Title: Coalescence of Emulsified Oily Wastewater by Fibrous Beds

Report No. and Date: Presented at the 30th Annual Purdue Industrial Waste Conference, Purdue University, Lafayette, Ind., May 6, 1975

Authors: J.-N. Chieu, E. F. Gloyna, and R. S. Schechter

Manufacturer of Equipment: Laboratory prototype

Design Features: System is a 2-foot-long Plexiglas cylindrical column, housing coalescing media. Three types of media were used: polyester felt, polypropylene felt, and glass mats.

Wastewater Characteristics: Influents were prepared by emulsifying oil and tap water in a household blender, stabilizing the mixture in an ultrasonic disrupter, and stirring continuously before use. Oils tested include refinery slop oil (coker slop oil and API skimmings) and No. 2 heating oil; the slop oils were filtered before use.

76

Method of Analysis: Oil content of all samples was measured using a Beckman Total Carbon Analyzer. Prior to analysis, each sample was homogenized ultrasonically to insure representative sampling.

Results: With influent containing 100 ppm oil, the following efficiencies were achieved:

Glass mats   60%
Polypropylene felt   80%
Polyester felt   90%

Higher efficiencies were reached at low flow rates.

Critical Comments: Fibers preferentially wetted by the dispersed phase favor coalescence and exhibit lower head loss. Oil-removal efficiency increases about 10-15% after minimum oil saturation. Oil content of effluents is higher than the desired limit.

Title: Centrifuge Coalescer for Separating Oil from Water in Shipboard Applications

Report No. and Date: AD-764-006, February 1973

Authors: A. C. Harvey, A. R. Guzdar, V. K. Stokes, and A. T. Fisk

Manufacturer of Equipment: Foster-Miller Associates, Waltham, Mass. 02154

Design Features: System consists of a three-stage rotor comprising a primary stage, a swept vane separator to separate large drops; a closely spaced, axial-plate, spiral-wrap coalescer to coalesce the small drops; and a secondary-stage swept vane separator to collect and separate coalesced oil. The conical ends of the rotor contain blades and passageways that act as centrifugal pump and centripetal turbine elements, at the inlet and outlet ends, respectively.

Wastewater Characteristics: Oil/water mixtures of No. 2 and No. 4 fuel oils, Nigerian crude, and detergents were emulsified by passage through a centrifugal pump; oil emulsions had sizes ranging from 2 to 100 μ. Stability analyses indicated that mixtures were quite stable; after 120 hours, remaining oil droplets had diameters of 2 to 15 μ.

Methods of Analysis: Samples were analyzed for oil content by two methods: (1) integration of the drop-size distribution measured by a Coulter counter and (2) infrared spectrophotometry. Both measurement techniques gave about 75 to 80% of the "true" oil concentration in samples measured; concentrations measured by the Coulter counter were approximately 90% of the values obtained by infrared analysis.

Results: Test data indicated good separation with an average of approximately 100 ppm in effluents, with influents containing greater than 1% oil. Overall oil-removal efficiency was greater than 90%. Performance worsened when influents contained detergents.

Critical Comments: Device was adequately tested. Test procedure is satisfactory, and if improvements in design can be made, device is capable of achieving higher oil-removal efficiencies. Equipment is expensive. Effects of ship motion during processing were not investigated.

Cost: 100 gpm unit $22,900

Title: Development of a Centrifugal System for Separation of Oil and Solids from Shipboard Discharge Water

Report No. and Date: CG-D-118-75, July 1975

Authors: A. R. Guzdar, A. C. Harvey, J. Potter, and W. M. Mack

Manufacturer of Equipment: Foster-Miller Associates, Inc., 135 Second Avenue, Waltham, Mass. 02154

Design Features: Device is an oil/solids/water separating system made up of the following components: (1) a cleanable bag strainer to retain coarse and fibrous solids, (2) a centrifugal pump to separate settleable solids, (3) a coalescing centrifuge to separate well-dispersed oil, and (4) an oil/water monitor to continuously measure and record the oil content of effluent.

Wastewater Characteristics: Oil/water mixtures were emulsified by passage through a centrifugal pump operating at 30 psi pressure differential. Lube oil and No. 2 fuel oil were used. The oil concentration of influent streams varied from 5 to 100%.

Method of Analysis: An on-line oil/water monitor continuously measured and recorded the oil content of effluents. Analytical results compared favorably with results using EPA solvent extraction-spectrophotometric techniques.

Results: Laboratory testing of individual components showed favorable performance. However, the performance of the overall system was poor. Oil content of effluents was much higher than the expected upper limit of 15 ppm.

Critical Comments: The poor system performance was blamed on "certain operational difficulties" experienced during the testing program. Design modifications may improve performance.

Title: Bimetallic Coalescers: Electrophoretic Coalescence of Emulsions in Beds of Mixed Metal Granules

Report No. and Date: Environ. Sci. Technol., 4, No. 6, 510-514 (1970)

Authors: F. M. Fowkes, F. W. Anderson, and J. E. Berger

Manufacturer of Equipment: A laboratory prototype assembled by authors

Design Features: Device is a cylindrical column packed with carbon (4-8-mesh size) and aluminum (20-mesh size) granules.

Wastewater Characteristics: Influents contained oil-in-water emulsions. Methods of preparation of feed streams were not stated.

Method of Analysis: Influent and effluent samples were analyzed for oil content by light transmission.

Results: Light transmission data indicate some separation occurred, with influents containing as much as 1100 ppm oil; coalescence was faster as influents became more dilute.

Critical Comments: Performance is poor and device is not adequate as a polishing stage in a treatment process. Consumption of metals is a problem. Further treatment is a necessity.

Title: Oil Removal by Carbon-Metal Granular Beds

Report No. and Date: J. Water Poll. Control Fed., 47, No. 8, 2101-2113 (1975)

Authors: M. M. Ghosh and W. P. Brown

Manufacturer of Equipment: Bench-scale coalescer assembled by authors

Design Features: Device consists of a glass column packed with a mixture of carbon and metal granules, supported by a 40-mesh metal screen. Activated cocoanut charcoal and aluminum or iron were used as bed materials.

Wastewater Characteristics: Stable emulsions of oil droplets in water were obtained when small volumes of solutions of silicone oil in acetone were jetted into water, through a small orifice. In some experiments, a homogenizer was used, at speeds of 12,000 rpm for 12 minutes, in preparing oil-in-water emulsions. Dispersions were less than 1.0μ in diameter and did not exhibit any self-coalescence over long periods of time.

Methods of Analysis: Influent and effluent samples were analyzed for number and size distribution of oil droplets by a particle counter. Spectrophotometric analyses of some samples were carried out.

Results: The highest oil-removal efficiency achieved, with influents containing approximately 350 ppm oil, was 82%.

Critical Comments: Analytical methods are only accurate to within 50% of actual value. Throughput is small and head loss gradually increased during processing. Formation of metal hydroxides that dissolve in effluent is a disadvantage. The carbon-aluminum system performed better than the carbon-iron system, because of the higher potential difference of the bimetallic couple. Bimetallic coalescers can be used only as polishing devices in oil/water separation, and are useful for separating oil dispersions stabilized by surface charges.

Title: The Coanda-Effect Oil-Water Separator: A Feasibility Study

Report No. and Date: AD-774-080, February 1974 (NTIS)

Author: D. Pal

Manufacturer of Equipment: Experimental model designed by Civil Engineering
                            Laboratory, Port Hueneme, Calif. 93043

Design Features: Device consists of inlet and outlet ports, 12-inch-long attachment wall, oil-collection chambers, and oil/water interface detection probes. Housing was made of Plexiglas to allow visual observation.

Wastewater Characteristics: The oil/water mixture used as influent was prepared by mixing hydraulic oil and tap water.

Method of Analysis: Volumes of oil and water present in settled samples were measured.

Results: Test data show that about 50% of the oil present in the influent was separated; the separated oil contained up to 5% free water.

Critical Comments: The Coanda-effect separator is in a developmental stage; it is useful only for gross separations. Turbulence created by jet flow will enhance emulsification of oil in wastewater, making separation very difficult.

SECTION 8

SELECTED MANUFACTURERS OF OIL/WATER SEPARATING EQUIPMENT

Gravity-Differential Separators

Aerodyne Development Corporation, Cleveland Ohio
AFL Industries, West Chicago, Illinois
Aqua-Chem, Inc., Waukesha, Wisconsin
Butterworth Systems, Inc., Bayonne, New Jersey
C. E. NATCO, Tulsa, Oklahoma
Chiyoda Chemical Engineering & Construction Company, Ltd., Tokyo
De Laval Separator Company, Poughkeepsie, New York
Envirex, Inc., Waukesha, Wisconsin
FMC Corporation, Lansdale, Pennsylvania
Fram-Akers Corporation, Tulsa, Oklahoma
FWI, Pollution Control Division, Tulsa, Oklahoma
General Electric Corporation, Philadelphia, Pennsylvania
Heil Process Equipment Corporation, Cleveland, Ohio
Inland Environmental, Chicago, Illinois
MAPCO, Inc., Tulsa, Oklahoma
Midland-Ross, Roxboro, North Carolina
The Permutit Company, Paramus, New Jersey
Pielkenroad Separator Company, Houston, Texas
Separator & Recovery Systems, Inc., Santa Ana, California
Smith Industries, Inc., Houston, Texas

Flotation Equipment

Ecodyne Corporation, Union, New Jersey
Envirex, Inc., Waukesha, Wisconsin
FWI, Pollution Control Division, Tulsa, Oklahoma
The Galigher Company, Salt Lake City, Utah
Joy Manufacturing Company, Denver, Colorado
Lockheed Aircraft Service Company, Ontario, Canada
Mechanics Research, Inc., Los Angeles, California
The Permutit Company, Paramus, New Jersey
Petrolite Corporation, Tretolite Division, St. Louis, Missouri

Rotational Equipment

Air Research Manufacturing Company, Torrance, California
Ametek, Inc., East Moline, Illinois
Centrico, Inc., Northvale, New Jersey
De Laval Separator Company, Poughkeepsie, New York
Foster-Miller Associates, Waltham, Massachusetts

81

Pennwalt Corporation, Warminster, Pennsylvania
Reynolds Submarine Service Company, Richmond, Virginia
Sharples Division, Pennwalt Corporation, North White Plains, New York
United Aircraft Corporation, East Hartford, Connecticut

Filtration Equipment (granular media)

Combustion Engineering Company, East Hartford, Connecticut
De Laval Separator Company, Poughkeepsie, New York
Hayward Filter Company, Santa Ana, California
Neptune Micro-Floc, Inc., Corvallis, Oregon
Peabody Welles, Roscoe, Illinois
Smith Industries, Inc., Houston, Texas

Filter/Coalescers

Aqua-Chem, Inc., Waukesha, Wisconsin
Fram-Akers Corporation, Tulsa, Oklahoma
FWI, Tulsa, Oklahoma
Inland Environmental, Chicago, Illinois
MAPCO, Inc., Tulsa, Oklahoma
Midland-Ross Corporation, Roxboro, North Carolina
Pall Trincor Corporation, Vauxhall, New Jersey
Selas Flotronics, Spring House, Pennsylvania
Separator & Recovery Systems, Inc., Santa Ana, California
Serfilco, Northbrook, Illinois
Smith Industries, Inc., Houston, Texas
Velcon Filters, Inc., San Jose, California

Membrane Filtration Equipment

Abcor, Inc., Cambridge, Massachusetts
Aqua-Media, Sunnyvale, California
Fluid Systems Division, UOP, Inc., San Diego, California
Gulf Environmental Systems, San Diego, California
Illinois Water Treatment Company, Rockford, Illinois
Osmonics, Inc., Hopkins, Minnesota
Romicon, Inc., Woburn, Massachusetts
Selas Flotronics, Spring House, Pennsylvania

Adsorption Equipment

APV Company, Inc., Tonawanda, New York
Aqua-Media, Sunnyvale, California
Calgon Corporation, Pittsburgh, Pennsylvania
Chem-Pro Equipment Corporation, Fairfield, New Jersey
Chiyoda Chemical Engineering & Construction Company, Ltd., Tokyo
Diamond Shamrock, Cleveland, Ohio
Ecodyne Corporation, Union, New Jersey
Envirex, Inc., Conshohocken, Pennsylvania
General Filter Company, Ames, Iowa
Hydronautics, Inc., Laurel, Maryland

Illinois Water Treatment Company, Rockford, Illinois
Liquitech, Inc., Houston, Texas
Met-Pro Systems, Inc., Lansdale, Pennsylvania
Process Equipment Corporation, Bedding, Michigan
Serfilco, Northbrook, Illinois

SECTION 9

REFERENCES

Adamson, A. W. (1967) Physical Chemistry of Surfaces. 2nd ed. Interscience, New York. 747 pp.

Adamson, W. L., and M. W. Titus (1971) Separation of oil in bilge water by semipermeable membrane. Naval Ship Research and Development Center Rept. No. AD-AO23-289, NTIS.

API (1969) Manual on Disposal of Refinery Wastes: Volume on Liquid Wastes. 1st ed. American Petroleum Institute, Washington, D. C.

Arnaiz, J. B., and E. Batutis (1974) Feasibility test program of application of coalescing phase oil/water separators to self-compensating fuel tanks in surface ships. U.S. Coast Guard Rept. No. CG-D-88-74, NTIS.

Berry, W. L., and R. F. Engel (1969) One approach minimizes water pollution from offshore platforms. Pet. Eng., 10:64-66.

Beychok, M. R. (1973) Aqueous Wastes from Petroleum and Petrochemical Plants. J. Wiley and Sons, New York.

Boehm, P. D. (1973) Solubilization of hydrocarbons by dissolved organic matter in seawater. M.S. Thesis. University of Rhode Island, Kingston.

Boehm, P. D., and J. G. Quinn (1974) The solubility behavior of No. 2 fuel oil in seawater. Mar. Poll. Bull., 5(7):101-105.

Boesch, D. F., C. H. Hershner, and J. H. Milgram (1974) Oil Spills and the Marine Environment. Ballinger Publishing Co., Cambridge, Mass.

Brunsmann, J. J., J. Cornelissen, and H. Eilers (1962) Improved oil separation in gravity separators. J. WPCF, 34(1):44-55.

Budininkas, P., and G. A. Remus (1974) Development of classification scale for characterizing bilge waters used in evaluating oil removal techniques. U.S. Coast Guard Report No. AD-778-929, NTIS.

Burtis, T. A., and C. G. Kirkbride (1946) Desalting of petroleum by use of fiberglass packing. Trans. AIChE., 42:413-416.

Chieu, J.-N., E. F. Gloyna, and R. S. Schechter (1975) Coalescence of emulsified oily wastewater by fibrous beds. Presented at the 30th Industrial Waste Conference, Purdue University, Lafayette, Ind.

84

Chiyoda Company (1974) Water treatment technologies from Chiyoda. Tech. Rept. No. 209-04, Chiyoda Company, Tokyo.

Churchill, R. J. (1973) Air flotation techniques for oily water treatment. Tech. Rept., Engineering Science, Inc., Pasadena, Calif.

Churchill, R. J., and W. J. Kaufman (1973) Waste processing related surface chemistry of oil refinery wastewaters. SERL Rept. No. 73-3, University of California, Berkeley.

D'Arcy, N. A. (1951) Dissolved air flotation separates oil from wastewater. Oil Gas J., 6:319-322.

Desai, S. V. (1971) An economically attractive application of reverse osmosis to refinement of a petrochemical effluent stream. AIChE Symp. Ser., Water. pp. 379-387.

Douglas, E., and I. G. Elliot (1962) Developments in oily-water separator design. Trans. Inst. Mar. Eng., 74:164-168.

Ellis, M. M., and P. W. Fisher (1970) Clarifying oil field and refinery wastewaters by gas flotation. J. Pet. Technol. and Soc. Pet. Engrs. Rept. No. SPE 3198.

Elworthy, P. H., A. T. Florence, and C. B. Macfarlane (1968) Solubilization by Surface Active Agents. Chapman and Hall, Ltd., London. pp. 11-116.

Evers, R. H. (1975) Mixed-media filtration of oily wastewaters. J. Pet. Technol., 2:157-163.

Farley, R., and F. H. H. Valentin (1965) Coagulation as a means of separating oil from effluents. AIChE-IEC Symp. Ser., 1(1):15-20.

Finger, S. M., and R. B. Tabakin (1973) Development of shipboard oil/water separation systems. Rept. No. 73-ENAs-38, ASME, New York.

Finger, S. M., and T. S. Yu (1972) Technologies for shipboard oil pollution abatement: Effects of operational parameters on coalescence. Naval Ship Research and Development Center Rept. No. 3598.

Finger, S. M., and T. S. Yu (1973) Analytical examination of oil/water separation by coalescence. USEPA Control Technology Research and Development. pp. 403-408. Also in Proceedings of the Joint Conference on Prevention and Control of Oil Spills. API, Washington, D. C. pp. 407-408.

Fowkes, F. M., F. W. Anderson, and J. E. Berger (1970) Bimetallic coalescers: Electrophoretic coalescence of emulsions in beds of mixed metal granules. Env. Sci. Technol., 4(6):510-514.

Freestone, F. J., and R. B. Tabakin (1975) Review of Environmental Protection Agency research in oil/water separation technology. Proceedings of the Joint Conference on Prevention and Control of Oil Spills. API, Washington, D. C. pp. 437-441.

Fruman, D. H. (1974) Development of a batchwise in-situ regeneration-type separator to remove oil from oil-water suspensions. Tech. Rept. No. 7080-3, Hydronautics, Inc., Maryland.

Fruman, D. H., and T. R. Sundaram (1974) Evaluation of pump emulsification characteristics. Naval Ship Engineering Rept. No. 6159-00, NTIS.

Gaudin, A. M. (1957) Flotation. 2nd ed. McGraw-Hill Book Co., New York.

Ghosh, M. M., and W. P. Brown (1975) Oil removal by carbon-metal granular beds. J. WPCF, 47(8):2101-2113.

Cloyna, E. F., and D. L. Ford (1974) Control of refinery and petrochemical wastewaters and residuals. Presented at the 1st International Symposium on the Techniques of Liquid-Liquid Separation. Lamar University, Beaumont, Texas.

Goldsmith, R. L., and S. Hossain (1973) Ultrafiltration concept for separating oil from water. U.S. Coast Guard Rept. No. 4305.2/2, NTIS AD-758-318.

Graham, R. J. (1962) Separation of immiscible liquids by gravity settling and induced coalescence. M.S. Thesis. University of California, Berkeley.

Gudesen, R. C. (1964) Coalescence of petroleum compounds in mixed fibrous beds. M.S. Thesis. Illinois Institute of Technology, Chicago.

Guzdar, A. R., A. C. Harvey, J. Potter, and W. M. Mack (1975) Development of a centrifugal system for separation of oil and solids from shipboard discharge water. U.S. Coast Guard Rept. No. CG-D-118-75, NTIS.

Harris, F. R., Inc. (1973) Port collection and separation facilities for oily wastes. II. General technology. Maritime Administration Rept. No. COM-73-11069, NTIS.

Hartenstein, L. J., and T. E. Lindemuth (1970) Development of a coalescing type oil/water separator for marine service. Aqua-Chem Tech. Rept. presented at SNAME Meeting, San Diego, California, February 18.

Harvey, A. C., A. R. Guzdar, V. K. Stokes, and A. T. Fisk (1973) Centrifuge coalescer for separating oil from water in shipboard applications. U.S. Coast Guard Rept. No. AD-764-006, NTIS.

Hayes, J. G., L. A. Hays, and H. S. Wood (1949) Commercial desalting unit employing fiberglass as contacting agent. Chem. Eng. Progr. 45:235.

Hazlett, R. N. (1969a) Fibrous bed coalescence of water: Steps in the coalescence process. IEC, Fund., 8(4):625-632.

Hazlett, R. N. (1969b) Fibrous bed coalescence of water: Role of sulfonate surfactant in the coalescence process. IEC, Fund., 8(4):633-640.

Hefler, J. R. (1971) Oily water separator: Liquid-liquid separation by a commercial self-cleaning edge filter. Maritime Administration Rept. No. COM-71-01095, NTIS.

Holt, Ben Company, The (1974) Experimental prototype oily wastewater treatment system. Civil Engineering Lab. Rept. No. CR-74.008, NTIS.

Hooper, M. W., and H. N. Myrick (1972) Comparison of multi-media and deep-bed sand filter coalescence of oil-water emulsions. Presented at Conference on Application of Filtration Technology in Environmental Pollution Control and the Chemical Process Industries. University of Houston, Texas.

Hsiung, K. Y., H. M. Mueller, and W. R. Conley (1974) Physical-chemical treatment for oily waste. Presented at WWEMA Industrial Water and Pollution Conference and Exposition, Detroit, Mich.

Ingersoll, A. C. (1951) Fundamentals and performance of gravity separation. Pet. Refiner, 6:9.

Jefferson, T. H., and S. B. Boulavare (1973) Surfactants and their effects on filter separators. U.S. Army Mobility Equipment Research and Development Center Rept. No. 2066, NTIS.

Jeffreys, G. V., and G. A. Davies (1971) Coalescence of liquid droplets and liquid dispersion. In: Recent Advances in Liquid-Liquid Extraction (C. Hanson, Ed.). Pergamon Press, Oxford. pp. 561-562.

Jordan, G. V. (1953) Separation of immiscible liquids by means of porous membranes. Trans. ASME, 77:393-404.

Jordan, G. V. (1965) Coalescence of fluids through porous materials. Selas Corporation Tech. Bull. LFC. Selas Corporation of America, Flotronics, Spring House, Pa.

Kaiser, R., C. K. Colton, G. Miskolczy, and L. Mir (1971) Magnetically induced separation of stable emulsions. AIChE Symp. Ser., Water. pp. 115-126.

Kirby, A. W. W. (1964) The separation of petroleum oils from aqueous effluents. Trans. Inst. Chem. Eng. (London), 4a(4):76.

Koelmans, H., and J. T. G. Overbeek (1954) Stability and electrophoretic deposition of suspensions in non-aqueous media. Dis. Faraday Soc., 18:52.

Kruyt, H. R. (1952) Colloid Science. Vol. 1. Elsevier, New York.

Lai, M. G., and C. E. Adams (1974) Determination of the molecular solubility of Navy oils in water. Naval Ordnance Lab. Rept. No. NOLTR-74-110, NTIS.

Langdon, W. M., P. P. Naik, and D. T. Wasan (1972) Separation of oil dispersions from water by fibrous bed coalescers. Env. Sci. Technol., 6(10):907.

Langdon, W. M., and D. T. Wasan (1971) Experimental evaluation of fibrous bed coalescers for separating oil-water emulsions. USEPA Project No. 12050 DRC.11/71, NTIS.

Lindenhofen, H., and R. H. Shertzer (1967) Aeronautical Engineering Lab. Rept. Nos. NAEC-AEL-1852 and NAEC-AEL-1856. Aeronautical Engineering Lab., Philadelphia, Pa.

Lysyj, I., and E. C. Russell (1974) Dissolution of petroleum-derived products in water. Water Res., 8:863-868.

McAuliffe, C. (1969a) Solubility in water of normal C_9 and C_{10} alkane hydrocarbons. Science, 163:478-479.

McAuliffe, C. (1969b) Determination of dissolved hydrocarbons in subsurface brines. Chem. Geol., 4:225-233.

McKenna, Q. H., H. Helber, C. M. Carrell, and R. F. Tobias (1973) Electrochemical flotation concept for removing oil from water. U.S. Coast Guard Rept. No. 734305.2/4, NTIS.

Mensing, A. E., R. C. Stoeffler, W. R. Davison, and T. E. Hoover (1970) Investigation of the use of a vortex flow to separate oil from an oil/water mixture. U.S. Coast Guard Rept. No. 714103/A/001, NTIS.

Merryman, J. G., and E. R. Osterstock (1973) Coalescing plates and packs for oil/water separation in various shipboard applications. U.S. Coast Guard Rept. No. 724305.2/6, NTIS.

Messinger, S. (1974) Ultrafiltration in water and waste treatment. Presented at the 12th Annual Liberty Bell Corrosion Course No. 4.

Milstead, C. E., and J. F. Loos (1973) Study of hydrophilic membranes for oil-water separation. U.S. Coast Guard Rept. No. 4305.2/7, NTIS AD-758-321.

Mittleman, J. (1975) Oil/water separator evaluation. Naval Coastal Systems Lab. Rept. No. 252-75, NTIS.

Navy, Department of the (1974) Coanda-effect oil-water separation. U.S. Department of the Navy, Washington, D. C., NTIS AD-D001-437.

Nordstrom, R. P., Jr. (1974) Ultrafiltration removal of soluble oil. Poll. Eng., 10:46-47.

Norton, L. B. (1972) Test and evaluation of oil pollution abatement devices for shipboard use. Phase II. U.S. Coast Guard Rept. No. AD-762-499, NTIS.

Norton, L. B., and F. Perrini (1972) Test and evaluation of oil pollution abatement devices for shipboard use. Phase I. U.S. Coast Guard Rept. No. AD-&62-498, NTIS.

Norton, L. B. (1973) Test and evaluation of oil pollution abatement devices for shipboard use. Phase III. Final U.S. Coast Guard Rept. No. AD-762-488, NTIS.

Orr, C., and E. Kang (1974) The electrical process in the breaking of dilute oil-in-water emulsions. Office of Water Resources Research Rept. No. PB-235-908, NTIS.

Overbeek, J. T. G. (1952) Colloid Science. Vol. I (H. R. Kruyt, Ed.). Elsevier, New York.

Pal, D. (1974) The Coanda-effect oil-water separator: A feasibility study. Civil Engineering Lab. Rept. No. AD-774-080, NTIS.

Paszyc, A. J., D. Pal, K. Huang, and J. B. Curry (1975) Fluidic oil-water separator. U.S. Department of the Navy, Washington, D. C., NTIS AD-D001-756.

Pomonik, G. M. (1973) Vacuum desorption concept for removing oil from water. U.S. Coast Guard Rept. No. 734305.2/8, NTIS.

Pontello, A. P., F. G. Woessner, and R. J. Delfosse (1973) Oil/water pollution program. Phase I. Naval Air Propulsion Test Center Rept. No. NAPTC-PE-27, NTIS.

Pontello, A. P., C. J. Collick, J. J. Palmer, and A. J. Rollo (1974) Oil/water pollution program. Phase II. U.S. Department of the Navy, Washington, D. C., NTIS AD-A009-093.

Quigley, R. E., and E. L. Hoffman (1966) Flotation of oil wastes. Proceedings of the 21st Industrial Waste Conference. Purdue University, Lafayette, Ind. pp. 527-533.

Redmon, O. C. (1963) Cartridge type coalescers. Chem. Eng. Progr., 59(9):87.

Reisberg, J., and T. M. Doscher (1956) Interfacial phenomena in crude oil-water systems. Producers Monthly, 4:43.

Rohlich, G. A. (1951) Hydraulic characteristics of gravity-type oil-water separators. Proc. API, 31M(111):63-85.

Rohlich, G. A. (1954) Application of air flotation to refinery wastewaters. Ind. Eng. Chem., 46(2):304-308.

Rose, P. R. (1963) Mechanisms of operation of a fibrous bed coalescer. M.S. Thesis. Illinois Institute of Technology, Chicago, Ill.

Rosenfeld, J. I., and D. T. Wasan (1974) Coalescence of drops in a liquid-liquid dispersion by passage through a fibrous bed. Can. J. Chem. Eng., 52:26-34.

Russell, E. C. (1972) Test and evaluation of a 50-gallon-per-minute oil/water separator (Separation and Recovery Systems, Inc.). U.S. Army Mobility Equipment Research and Development Center Rept. No. AD-785-223, NTIS.

Russell, E. C. (1973a) RPC Division, Midland-Ross Corporation 10-gallon-per-minute liquid/liquid separator. U.S. Army Mobility Equipment Research and Development Center Rept. No. 2058, NTIS.

Russell, E. C. (1973b) Fram Corporation Model OWS-23-FCI-USCG oil/water separator. U.S. Army Mobility Equipment Research and Development Center Rept. No. 2059, NTIS.

Russell, E. C. (1973c) Separation and Recovery Systems, Inc. 100-gallon-per-minute oil/water separator. U.S. Army Mobility Equipment Research and Development Center Rept. No. 2060, NTIS.

Sareen, S. S., P. M. Rose, R. C. Gudesen, and R. C. Kintner (1966) Coalescence in fibrous beds. AIChE J., 12:1045.

SCEP (1970) Man's Impact on the Global Environment: Report of the Study of Critical Environmental Problems. MIT Press, Cambridge, Mass. 296 pp.

Schatzberg, P., L. R. Harris, C. M. Adema, D. F. Jackson, and C. M. Kelly (1975) Oil-water separation with noncellulosic ultrafiltration systems. Proceedings of the Joint Conference on Prevention and Control of Oil Spills. API, Washington, D. C. pp. 443-447.

Shackleton, L. R. B., E. Douglas, and T. Walsh (1960) Pollution of the sea by oil. Trans. Inst. Mar. Eng.

Sheng, H. P., and J. R. Welker (1969) Liquid-liquid separation in a conventional hydrocyclone. Proceedings of the AIChE 64th National Meeting, New Orleans, La.

Sherony, D. F., and R. C. Kintner (1971) Coalescence of an emulsion in a fibrous bed. II. Experimental. Can. J. Chem. Eng., 49:321.

Simonsen, R. N. (1962) Remove oil by air flotation. Hydrocarbon Proc. and Pet. Ref., 41:5.

Sims, A. V. (1972) Test and evaluation of oil-water separation systems. Naval Civil Engineering Lab. Rept. No. CR-73-015, NTIS.

Sinkin, D. J., and R. B. Olney (1956) Phase separation and mass transfer in a liquid-liquid cyclone. AIChE J., 2(4):545-551.

Skocypec, R. J. (1972) Oily water separation system. U.S. Maritime Administration Rept. No. COM-72-10561, NTIS.

Spielman, L. A. (1968) Separation of finely dispersed liquid-liquid suspensions by flow through fibrous media. Ph.D. Dissertation. University of California, Berkeley.

Spielman, L. A., and S. L. Goren (1970) Progress in induced coalescence and a new theoretical framework for coalescence by porous media. Ind. Eng. Chem., 62(10):10-24.

Spielman, L. A., and S. L. Goren (1972a) Theory of coalescence by flow through porous media. Ind. Eng. Chem., Fund., 11(1):66.

Spielman, L. A., and S. L. Goren (1972b) Experiments in coalescence by flow through fibrous mats. Ind. Eng. Chem., Fund., 11(1):73.

Stoeffler, R. C., and C. E. Jones (1973) Vortex concept for separating oil from water. U.S. Coast Guard Rept. No. 4105.2/1, NTIS.

Stormont, D. H. (1956) Air flotation used to separate oil at Richfield's new waste water plant. Oil Gas J., 10:26.

Sweeney, W. F. (1964) Some observations on liquid-liquid settling. M.S. Thesis. University of California, Berkeley.

Union Carbide Corporation (1973) Viscosity-actuated phase separating (VAPS) for oil-water separations. Prepared for U.S. Coast Guard, Rept. No. 734305.2/5, NTIS.

USEPA (1974) Development document for effluent limitations guidelines and new source performance standards for petroleum refining: Point source category. USEPA No. 440/1-74-014a, NTIS.

USEPA (1975) Group II. Development document for interim final effluent limitations guidelines and new source performance standards for the offshore segment of the oil and gas extraction point source category. USEPA No. 440/1-75-055, NTIS.

Vinson, C. G. (1965) The coalescence of micro-size drops in liquid-liquid dispersions in flow past fine mesh screens. Ph.D. Dissertation. University of Michigan, Ann Arbor.

Voyutskii, S. S., K. A. Kal'yanova, R. Panick, and N. Fodiman (1955) Mechanism of separation of the dispersed phase of emulsions during filtration. Chem. Abstr., 49:12053d.

Voyutskii, S. S., N. M. Fodiman, and R. Panick (1958) Filtration of emulsions. Chem. Abstr., 52:19266a.

Vrablik, E. R. (1957) An evaluation of circular gravity-type separators and dissolved air flotation for treating oil refinery waste water.

Proceedings of the 12th Industrial Waste Conference. Purdue University, Lafayette, Ind. p. 73.

Wang, L. K., J. Y. Yang, and D. B. Dohm (1973) Evaluation and development of physical-chemical techniques for the separation of emulsified oil from water. Rept. No. 189, Calspan Corporation, Buffalo, N. Y.

Wisconsin, University of (1949) Investigation of the behavior of oil-water mixtures in separators. Eng. Expt. Sta. Ser. Rept. No. CE-78-1. University of Wisconsin, Madison.

Wisconsin, University of (1950) Investigation of the behavior of oil-water mixtures in separators. Eng. Expt. Sta. Ser. Rept. No. CE-78-2. University of Wisconsin, Madison.

Wisconsin, University of (1951) Investigation of the behavior of oil-water mixtures in separators. Eng. Expt. Sta. Ser. Rept. No. CE-78-3. University of Wisconsin, Madison.

Yu, T. S. (1969) A proposed shipboard continuous oil-pollution control process for bilge water. Naval Ship Research and Development Lab. Rept. No. 3191, NTIS.

Yu, T. S., and D. R. Ventriglio (1969) Shipboard oil-pollution control systems for ballast and bilge waters: A state-of-the-art search. MATLAB Rept. No. 244, NTIS.

SECTION 10

BIBLIOGRAPHY

Armco Steel Corporation. 1970. Treatment of Waste Water: Waste Oil Mixtures. Federal Water Pollution Control Administration Program No. 12010 EZV.

Battelle Memorial Laboratory (Pacific Northwest Laboratory). 1967. Oil Spillage Study: Literature Search and Critical Evaluation for Selection of Promising Techniques to Control and Prevent Damage. NTIS Rept. No. AD-666-289.

Beebe, A. H. 1953. Soluble Oil Wastes Treatment by Pressure Flotation. Sewage Ind. Wastes. 25(11):1314-1322.

Blumer, M. 1969. Oil Pollution of the Ocean. In: Oil on the Sea. Ed. D. P. Hoult. Plenum Press, New York. pp. 5-13.

Blumer, M. 1970. Scientific Aspects of the Oil Spill Problem. Presented at the Colloquium on Oil Pollution of the Sea. North Atlantic Treaty Organization, Brussels.

Boyd, J. L., G. L. Shell, and D. A. Dahlstrom. 1972. Treatment of Oily Waste Waters to Meet Regulatory Standards. AIChE Symp. Ser. 124:393-401.

Breslau, B. R., E. A. Agranat, A. J. Testa, S. Messinger, and R. A. Cross. 1974. Hollow Fiber Ultrafiltration: A Systems Approach for Process Water and By-Product Recovery. Proceedings of the AIChE 79th National Meeting, Houston, Texas.

Brown and Root, Inc. 1974. Determination of Best Practicable Control Technology Currently Available to Remove Oil from Water Produced with Oil and Gas. Offshore Operators Committee, Sheen Technical Subcommittee Report.

Canadian Plant and Process Engineering, Ltd. 1972. Polyurethane as an Oil Filter: A Research Study. Final Report, Canadian Department of the Environment (Fisheries and Forestry), Ontario.

Canevari, G. P. 1969. Some Basic Concepts Regarding the Separation of Oily Water Mixtures. Trans. ASCE. 12:190.

Cheesman, D. F., and A. King. 1940. The Electrical Double Layer in Relation to the Stabilization of Emulsions with Electrolytes. Trans. Faraday Soc. 36:241.

Chemical Engineering Deskbook. 1975. Environmental Engineering Pollution Control Equipment. 82(21). McGraw-Hill Book Co., Hightstown, N. J.

Chieu, J. N., and E. F. Gloyna. 1975. Treatment of Emulsified Oily Wastes by Fibrous Bed Coalescers. CRWR Report, University of Texas, Austin.

Conley, W. R., and K. Hsiung. 1969. Design and Application of Multi-media Filters. J. Amer. Water Works Assn. 61:97.

Degler, S. E. 1970. Oil Pollution: Problems and Policies. BNA's Environmental Management Series.

Edwards, V. H., and R. K. Finn. 1969. New Separation Techniques. AIChE, Today Series, New Orleans, La. pp. 21-22.

Engineering Science, Inc. (Texas). 1971. Preliminary Investigational Requirements: Petrochemical and Refinery Waste Treatment Facilities. EPA Project No. 12020 EID, NTIS.

Gloyna, E. F., and D. L. Ford. 1970. The Characteristics and Pollutional Problems Associated with Petrochemical Wastes. Engineering Science, Inc., Texas, Report.

Goldsmith, R. L., and S. Hossain. 1973. Oil-Water Separation by Ultrafiltration. Proceedings of the Joint Conference on Prevention and Control of Oil Spills. API, Washington, D. C. pp. 441-456.

Goldsmith, R. L., D. A. Roberts, and D. L. Burre. 1974. Ultrafiltration of Soluble Oil Wastes. JWPCF. 46(9):2183-2192.

Goren, S. L. 1974. Removal of Oil from Aqueous Wastes by Flotation. Office of Water Resources Research, Washington, D. C. Rept. No. PB-234-023, NTIS.

Grosz, R. B., and R. A. Kormanck. 1975. Dissolved Air Flotation. Unpublished report.

Gruenfeld, M. 1973. Extraction of Dispersed Oils from Water for Quantitative Analysis by Infrared Spectrophotometry. Env. Sci. Technol. 7(7):636-639.

Hensen, S. P., G. H. Richardson, and K. Hsiung. 1969. Some Recent Advances in Water Treatment Technology. Chem. Eng. Progr., Symp. Ser. 65.

Harris, R. F. 1975. Report on Port Collection and Separation Facilities for Oily Wastes. Volume IV: Determination of Impact of the Construction of Offshore Terminals on Their Contiguous Ports. Maritime Administration Contract No. 2-36202, NTIS.

Harvey, A. C., A. R. Guzdar, and D. R. Friswell. 1973. Laboratory Evaluation of the Emulsifying Characteristics of Pumps. U.S. Coast Guard Rept. No. CG-D-31-74, NTIS.

Harvey, A. C., and V. K. Stokes. 1973. Evaluation of a Unique Centrifuge for Separation of Oil from Ship Discharge Waters. Proceedings of the Joint Conference on Prevention and Control of Oil Spills. API, Washington, D. C. p. 391.

Hoult, D. P. 1969. Oil on the Sea. Plenum Press, New York.

Hyland, J. R. 1971. Study of Oily Water Marine Treatment Facilities. USEPA Office of Water Programs Report, NTIS.

Jones, H. R. 1973. Pollution Control in the Petroleum Industry. Noyes Data Corporation, New Jersey.

King, A. 1941. Some Factors Governing the Stability of Oil-in-Water Emulsions. Trans. Faraday Soc. 37:168.

Lederman, P. B., and J. S. Dorrler. 1975. Development of Offshore Oil and Gas in New England: Environmental Problems and Solutions. USEPA Report.

Little, R. C. 1974. Breaking Emulsions of Water in Navy Fuel Oils. Fuel. 53:246-252.

McKay, W. C. 1973. Evaluation of Concepts for Separating Oil from Water Discharged from Ships. U.S. Coast Guard Rept. No. CG-D-26-74, NTIS 734305.2/9.

Milne, D. 1950. Character of Waste Oil Emulsions. Sewage Ind. Wastes. 22(3):326.

Nelson-Smith, A. 1972. Oil Pollution and Marine Ecology. Elek Science, London.

Permutit Company (The). 1966. Research and Development for a Shipboard Oil and Water Separation System. Maritime Administration Contract No. MA-2722, NTIS.

Poliakoff, M. Z. 1969. Oil Dispersing Chemicals. Federal Water Pollution Control Administration Rept. No. 15080FHS-05/69-14/12/549.

Pomeroy, R. 1953. Floatability of Oil and Grease in Wastewaters. Sewage Ind. Wastes. 25:1304-1313.

Redlien, W. H., and J. H. McClintock. 1951. Reducing Water Pollution for Oil Refineries. Pet. Refiner. 30(6):123-126.

Reid, G. W., L. E. Streebin, D. W. Rumfeldt, and R. Sweazy. 1972. Evaluation of Waste Waters from Petroleum and Coal Processing. EPA-R2,72-001.

Shah, D. O. 1970. Molecular Interactions at the Oil/Water Interfaces and the Formation of Microemulsions. Federal Water Pollution Control Administration Rept. No. 15080EMP-06/70.

Skocypec, R. 1974. Electrolyte Effects on Flotation of Oily Water. M.S. Thesis. University of California, Berkeley.

Smookler, A. L., and J. W. Harden. 1973. Navy Shipboard Investigation of Oily Wastes. Proceedings of the Joint Conference on Prevention and Control of Oil Spills. API, Washington, D. C. pp. 189-193.

Sniegoski, P. J. 1973. The Determination of Water Soluble Components in Petroleum Products Used by the Navy. U.S. Naval Research Laboratory 2nd Progress Report.

Sollner, S. 1944. The Application of Sonic and Ultrasonic Waves in Colloid Chemistry. Chem. Rev. 34:371.

Sport, M. C. 1969. Design and Operation of Gas Flotation Equipment for the Treatment of Oilfield Produced Brines. Presented at the Offshore Technology Conference, Houston, Texas. Preprint No. OTC 1051. 1:111-145.

Stahl, G. W., D. H. Meyer, and B. H. Rankin. 1972. Separation of Oil in Bilge Water by Semipermeable Membranes. Naval Systems Engineering Rept. No. USNA EW-72-7, NTIS.

Thompson, C. S., J. Stock, and P. L. Mehta. 1972. Cost and Operating Factors for Treatment of Oily Waste Water. Oil Gas J. 53.

Thompson, D. 1951. Ultrasoncs. Chem. Eng. Progr. Symp. Series. 47(1).

Vrablik, E. R. 1959. Fundamental Principles of Dissolved Air Flotation of Industrial Wastes. Proceedings of the 14th Industrial Waste Conference, Purdue University, Lafayette, Ind. p. 743.

Weston, R. F. 1950. Separation of Oil Refinery Wastes. Ind. Eng. Chem. 4.

Weston, R. F. 1952. Waste Control at Oil Refineries. Chem. Eng. Progr. 9.

Witmer, P. E., and A. Gollan. 1971. Oil-Water Regenerative Separator-- Phase I. Final Report of Phase I: Development Program of a Continuous Regenerative Moving Bed to Remove Oil from Oil-Water Suspensions. Maritime Administration Rept. No. COM-72-11041, NTIS.

TECHNICAL REPORT DATA
(Please read Instructions on the reverse before completing)

1. REPORT NO. EPA-600/2-78-069	2.	3. RECIPIENT'S ACCESSION NO.

4. TITLE AND SUBTITLE OIL/WATER SEPARATION: STATE-OF-THE-ART	5. REPORT DATE April 1978 issuing date
	6. PERFORMING ORGANIZATION CODE

7. AUTHOR(S) Fidelis A. Osamor / Robert C. Ahlert	8. PERFORMING ORGANIZATION REPORT NO.

9. PERFORMING ORGANIZATION NAME AND ADDRESS Dept. of Chemical & Biochemical Engineering Rutgers, The State University of New Jersey New Brunswick, New Jersey 08903	10. PROGRAM ELEMENT NO. EHE623
	11. CONTRACT/GRANT NO. R803978

12. SPONSORING AGENCY NAME AND ADDRESS Industrial Environmental Research Laboratory-Cin., OH Office of Research and Development U.S. Environmental Protection Agency Cincinnati, Ohio 45268	13. TYPE OF REPORT AND PERIOD COVERED Final 7/11/75 – 7/31/77
	14. SPONSORING AGENCY CODE EPA/600/12

15. SUPPLEMENTARY NOTES

16. ABSTRACT

This report reviews the state-of-the-art for oil/water separating devices and processes. Devices and process are classified according to the primary mechanism that induces separation of oil/water mixtures. The basic concepts, specific design features, operational conditions, and limitations of each category are discussed.

Literature on test evaluation of a variety of devices is critiqued on the basis of actual or potential success in treating various oil/water system states. No single technique can separate all oil/water system states efficiently. Specific deficiencies in existing technology have been identified.

This report was submitted in fulfillment of Research Grant No. R803978 by Rutgers University under the sponsorship of the U.S. Environmental Protection Agency. This report covers the period July 1, 1975, to June 30, 1977, and work was completed as of July 31, 1977.

17. KEY WORDS AND DOCUMENT ANALYSIS

a. DESCRIPTORS	b. IDENTIFIERS/OPEN ENDED TERMS	c. COSATI Field/Group
Petroleum industry Oil/water separation Oily wastewaters	Oil pollution Oil/water treatment Coalescence Gravity separation	68D

18. DISTRIBUTION STATEMENT – RELEASE TO PUBLIC	19. SECURITY CLASS *(This Report)* UNCLASSIFIED	21. NO. OF PAGES 104
	20. SECURITY CLASS *(This page)* UNCLASSIFIED	22. PRICE

EPA Form 2220-1 (9-73)

97